THE
POETIC
WORD

AN ANTHOLOGY OF POETRY
FOR THE SOUL

JOYCE A. BOAHENE

WESTBOW
P R E S S®
A DIVISION OF THOMAS NELSON
& ZONDERVAN

WestBow Press books may be ordered through booksellers or by contacting:

WestBow Press
A Division of Thomas Nelson & Zondervan
1663 Liberty Drive
Bloomington, IN 47403
www.westbowpress.com
844-714-3454

Because of the dynamic nature of the Internet, any web addresses or links contained in this book may have changed since publication and may no longer be valid. The views expressed in this work are solely those of the author and do not necessarily reflect the views of the publisher, and the publisher hereby disclaims any responsibility for them.

Any people depicted in stock imagery provided by Getty Images are models, and such images are being used for illustrative purposes only. Certain stock imagery © Getty Images.

Scripture quotations are taken from the New King James Version. Copyright © 1982 by Thomas Nelson, Inc. Used by permission. All rights reserved.

Scripture quotations marked AMP are taken from the Amplified® Bible, Copyright © 1954, 1958, 1962, 1964, 1965, 1987 by The Lockman Foundation. Used by permission.

ISBN: 978-1-6642-9091-4 (sc)
ISBN: 978-1-6642-9092-1 (hc)
ISBN: 978-1-6642-9090-7 (e)

Library of Congress Control Number: 2023901683

Print information available on the last page.

WestBow Press rev. date: 2/15/2023

I would like to dedicate this book to my three children. Adwoa, Afua, and Kwame, you have been my greatest blessings and inspiration. Over the years I have watched you grow in wisdom, maturity, and responsibility. I am very proud of you! I pray that you will continue to keep the faith. And may the Lord bless your lives and bring you into the fulfillment of your divine calling and destiny.

My heart is overflowing with a good theme; I recite my composition concerning the King; My tongue is the pen of a ready writer.
—Psalms 45:1

Contents

Poems of Heartfelt Prayers

Prayers of Encouragement/Comfort/Condolence

Poetic Notes from Heaven

Poems for the Church

Foreword

As our journey with the Lord moves forward in time, His special way of delivering blessings and words in due season becomes more apparent. This has always been true of our friend and sister in Christ Joyce Boahene. Her writings, whether in prose, verse, or any other format have become for us, "Like apples of gold in settings of silver" (Proverbs 25:11, AMP). They seem to always come at the proper time. What is the reason behind her great volume of work and creative output? It is due to nothing less than the time she spends at her Savior's feet, listening and considering every word that comes from His heart and into hers. You are about to be blessed!

Pastors Joe and Dawn Coudriet
Family Life Church
Vestal, New York 13850

Acknowledgments

I would like to acknowledge my Lord and Savior, Jesus Christ, for helping me to complete this second anthology of poetry. To all of my sisters in the Lord who have stood by and encouraged me along this journey; you have been a breath of fresh air! To my prayer partner Jacqueline Spears, thank you for being a friend who sticks closer than a brother! And thank you for helping me to proofread the manuscript. I would also like to acknowledge and honor my spiritual parents, Pastors Joe and Dawn Coudriet, for spurring me on and providing their endorsement for this book.

Introduction

Everyone has been given a free gift from God. Our responsibility is to find out what it is and use it for His glory and the benefit of society. Ephesians 2:10[1] says, "For we are His workmanship, created in Christ Jesus for good works, which God prepared beforehand that we should walk in them."

I have discovered that my gift is writing and creating framed pictures of my poetry. Poetry and prose is the unique way that God expresses His nature and character through me. My poetry speaks to the issues of life and harnesses the power of scriptures to soothe the soul and encourage and uplift people from every walk of life.

As a poet, I am aware that words have creative power, whether negative or positive. Kind words can bring comfort and healing. On the other hand, unkind words can cause emotional pain that lasts for a lifetime. I am thankful that God has given me the pen of a ready writer. So with this gift, I am committed to pen words that give readers a positive dose of inspiration and leave an indelible mark. I am reminded of a quote by Mother Teresa, which says, "I am a little pencil in the hand of a writing God who is sending a love letter to the world."

This second anthology of poetry includes themes of prayer, gratitude, and hope. The poems were not written in any particular order, but rather through some of the most challenging seasons of my life. It is my heartfelt prayer that this book blesses you whether you already know God or you are in active pursuit of Him. May each poem point you to God and bring a sense of comfort to your heart. Above all, may they spur you on your journey of life with a confident trust that God is your true help for today and your bright hope for the future.

---

[1]   Unless otherwise noted, all quotations from the Bible are taken from the New King James Version.

Writing and sowing seeds of goodness has been a major theme in my life. And I must say that even if no one else shows appreciation for what I do, I would still continue to sow and grow. However, over the years I have been blessed to have a faithful audience of people who regularly request my poetry for their homes, offices, or as gifts for someone who has mentored or inspired them. I have been told by a reader that my poetry is prophetic, that the words exhort, encourage, inspire, and rejuvenate both spirit and soul. I have also been told on countless occasions that my poetry expresses what is in a person's heart and should always be accompanied by a box of tissues. So welcome to my poetic garden where you will find warm inspirational words to nourish your soul.

God's joy is in my heart;
His pen is in my hand.
His words are on my lips.
Yes, everything that I have
Is truly a gift!

Poems of Gratitude

Oh, give thanks to the Lord, for He is good!
For His mercy endures forever.
—Psalm 118:29

A Room for God

I am building me a room for God,
And daily I am giving Him everything that I have.
I am building me a room for God.
And with a grateful heart
And my hands upraised,
I am offering Him the sacrifice of praise.

I am building me a room for God.
And I am receiving comfort
From His staff and rod.
I am building me a room for God,
For He is the greatest guest
That I will ever have.

I Thank You

Lord, I thank You for the blood on the mercy seat,
Where I can come and bow down at your feet.
Lord, I thank You for the blood on the mercy seat,
For it has cleansed and delivered me
And made me complete.
Lord, I thank You for the blood on the mercy seat,
For it has the power that no enemy can ever defeat.

I Am Climbing

I am climbing up on the mercy seat,
And with a heart of thanksgiving
I am coming daily to greet.

I am climbing up on the mercy seat,
And I am letting Jesus cleanse me
From the top of my head to the soles of my feet.

I am climbing up on the mercy seat,
For it is the place where my Savior
Has invited me to meet.

A Song of Praise

Lord, I am lifting up my voice
With a song of praise,
And I am coming to meet You face to face.

Lord, I am lifting up my voice
With a song of praise,
And I am honoring You daily
In all of my ways.

Lord, I am lifting up my voice
With a song of praise,
For it is a great weapon
That the enemy has no power to take.

I Lift Up My Hands

I lift up my hands and I give God the praise,
And I am asking Him to refine me
And reset my pace.

I lift up my hands and I give God the praise,
For this is no time to grow weary
And no time to waste.

I lift up my hands and I give God the praise,
And I am asking Him for a fresh anointing
For the direction where my life is pointing.

Your Glory

Lord, I thank You for your glory
That daily burns away the chaff.
Lord, I thank You for your glory
And my overcoming story.

Lord, I thank You for your creation
And your love for every nation.
Lord, I thank You for fresh revelation
And my daily transformation.

Lord, I thank You for your heavenly wisdom
And Your provision and protection.
Lord, I thank You for the Holy Ghost
That keeps leading me in the right direction.

I Am Thankful

Lord, I am thankful for the finished work
That You did upon Calvary.
I am thankful for your provision
And your daily acts of protection.

Lord, I am thankful for your amazing grace
That helps me to obey You
And stay strong in my race.

Thankful

Lord, I am thankful for your perfect love
And your bountiful blessings from above.
Lord, I am thankful for your faithfulness
In securing me a safe place to rest.

Lord, I am thankful for your amazing grace
And the courage that You give me
To keep running my race.
Lord, I am thankful for the unspeakable joy that You bring
When I am standing in the presence of the honorable King.

Father Thank You

Father, thank You for your steadfast love
And the mercy that You show me from heaven above.
Father, thank You for your precious Son
And the mighty things that He has done.
Father, thank You for your amazing grace
And another day to wake up and give You praise.

Today

Lord, today is another day for me
To pause and give You thanks.
It is a day to give thanks
For the air that I breathe;
It is a day to stop focusing
On the way that I feel.

Lord, today is another day for me
To pause and give You thanks.
It is a day to give thanks
For the food on my table.
It is a day to give thanks,
For You are the One who keeps me stable.

I Am Thanking God

I am thanking God for the flowers
That are beginning to bloom.
I am thanking Him for the ray of sunshine
That is replacing the gloom.

I am thanking God
That old man winter is walking out the door
And that good time summer is finally settling the score.

I am thanking God for the birds
That are circling the sky.
But this sunshine girl is looking out her window,
And she too is getting ready to fly.

Dear God

Dear God, when I reflect on my life
And your master plan,
I am in awe of the love
That You have bestowed from above.

When I consider the price
That your Son had to pay,
There is a force that compels me
To bow down and pray.

When I consider the frailness of humanity,
I am forever grateful for the treasure
That You have deposited in me.

Our Children

Lord, I thank You
That our children were not born for trouble,
For the blessings of the righteous
You have promised that You would double.

Lord, I thank You
That our children were not born for trouble,
For You are well able to keep them
From the depth of life's rubble.

Lord, I thank You
That our children were not born for trouble,
And they will never have to suffer
At the hands of the devil.

I Woke Up

I woke up this morning
To the humming of birds,
And oh what sweet melody
That my ears have just heard.

I woke up this morning
With a heart of thanksgiving,
And I choose to praise God
For the good life that I am living.

I woke up this morning
Under God's umbrella of love,
And I have an abiding peace
That comes only from the Father above.

Lord I Thank You

Lord, I thank You
For your steadfast love
And your mercy shown from heaven above.
Lord, I thank You for your precious Son
And the mighty works that He has done.

Lord, I thank You
For your amazing grace
And another day to wake up
And give You praise.

I Am Placing

Father, I am placing my life
In the palms of your hands,
For my care will never be left
To the mercy of man.

Father, I am placing my faith
In the finished work of your Son,
And I am thanking Him for the victory
That He has already won.

I Have Had

Lord, I thank You,
For though I fought a few battles
I still won the war.
And I found myself in love
With You more and more.

Lord, I have had a lot of questions,
And I have fought through some doubts
But ultimately, You were there
To work everything out.

Lord, I have had a few laughs,
And I did shed some tears
But You are the Good Shepherd
That has always been near.

Lord, I have had a few disappointments,
And I did feel some pain
But they have only elevated me
To a much higher plane.

The Greatest Friend

Lord, You are the greatest friend
That I have ever met.
You are my greatest teacher and advocate.

Lord, You are the only comforter
That soothes my soul.
You are my deliverer from the pain of old.

Lord, You are the faithful One
Who daily stands by me,
And I thank You for shedding your blood
Upon Calvary's tree.

If You Have

If you have breath in your lungs
And a place to lie down,
That is more than enough
To turn things around.

If you have food on the table
And a few dollars in the bank,
That is more than enough
For you to give thanks.

If you have clothes on your back
And God is your rock,
That is more than enough for you
To stay on the right track.

Lord Thank You

Lord, thank You
For your mercy and amazing grace.
Thank You for the courage to run
And stay strong in my race.

Lord, thank You
For providing my daily bread.
Thank You for every need
That You have faithfully met.

Lord, thank You
For divine healing and prosperity.
Lord, thank You
For my spiritual growth and maturity.

I Say Thank You

Lord, I lift up my voice,
And I give You thanks.
I say thank You for your steadfast love
And the mercy that You show me
From heaven up above.

Lord, I say thank You
For providing a secret place
Where I can meet with You daily face-to-face.

Lord, I say thank You
For suppling my daily bread
And giving me a life that is Spirit-led.

My New Attitude

Gratitude is my new attitude
That keeps on lifting me
To a higher altitude.

Gratitude opens my heart
To offer praise and thanksgiving.
Gratitude gives me a greater appreciation
For the blessed life that I am now living.

Give Thanks

Never forget to give thanks
For the food on your table.
Never forget to give thanks
To the God who is able.

Never forget to give thanks
For the air that you breathe.
Never forget to give thanks
When God supplies what you need.

Never forget to give thanks
To the One who is greater.
For His name is Emanuel
Our Lord and our Savior.

You Have Conquered

Lord, I thank You
That You have conquered every enemy
That will ever rise up to trouble me.

Lord, I thank You
That You have conquered every enemy
So that I can walk in the path of victory.

Lord, I thank You
That You have conquered every enemy,
And the fulfillment of my divine destiny
I will certainly see.

Lord I Am

Lord, I am thanking You
For divine health
And an open door of heaven's wealth.

Lord, I am thanking You
For a debt-free life
And for supernatural grace,
Where I no longer have to strive.

Lord, I am thanking You
For new covenant relationships
And a greater opportunity to serve You
With my spiritual gifts.

When I Consider

Lord, when I consider your plans
And the work of your hands,
I marvel at the mercy
That You have shown unto man.

Lord, when I consider your plans
And the work of your hands,
I am willing to trust You
When I cannot understand.

Lord, when I consider your plans
And the work of your hands,
I can only surrender
And say, yes, Lord, here I am.

I Am

Lord, I am thankful for the breath of life
And the opening up of my spiritual eyes.
Lord, I am thankful for my daily bread
And the precious blood
That You have shed.
Lord, I am thankful for the angelic host
And the power of the Holy Ghost.

That Secret Place

Lord, I am thankful
For that secret place
Where I can daily gaze
Upon your lovely face.

Lord, I am thankful
For that secret place
Where I can lie down and rest
From life's hurried pace.

Lord, I am thankful
For that secret place,
Which daily drips with the abundance
Of your mercy and grace.

You Have Given

Lord, You have given me the ability
To work and get wealth,
And You daily grant me great favor
In all of my labor.

Lord, You have given me the ability
To work and get wealth,
And to the number of my days
You have added good health.

Lord, You have given me the ability
To work and get wealth,
And your power and anointing
I have joyfully felt.

The Great Exchange

Lord, I thank You
For the great exchange
And your mercy and amazing grace.

Lord, I thank You
For the privilege of daily fellowship
And a life of genuine discipleship.

Today I Am Thankful

Today I am thankful for my daily bread
And God's Word through which my spirit is fed.
I am thankful for my daily bread
And a place where I can peacefully lay my head.

Today I am thankful for the upper room,
Where I can meet with my Savior
In the morning, evening, or at noon.

Psalm of Thanksgiving

Lord, I honor your name
On the face of this earth.
And I thank You, my Savior,
For such a new birth.

Lord, I thank You
For suppling my daily bread
And for the blood upon the cross
That You so willingly shed.

Lord, I thank You
For paying every debt that I owed
And the removal of every bad seed
That I have ever sowed.

Lord, I thank You
For giving me a heart to forgive
And for providing an example
Of how I should live.

Forever Thankful

I am thankful for the rising sun
And the mighty works
That God has done.

I am forever thankful for His provision
And His wisdom for every decision.
I am thankful for His throne of grace,
Where I find help to stay strong
In the course of my race.

I Am Inspired

I am inspired by the hands of God,
Who is the creator of every nation.
I am inspired by the very fact
That I am a part of His creation.

I am inspired by His unconditional love.
I am inspired by His Word.
I am inspired that His perfect plan
Has bought redemption for the fallen state of man.

Thanksgiving and Praise

My heart is overflowing
With thanksgiving and praise,
And my eyes are on the Author
And the Finisher of my faith.

My soul is in awe of His majesty,
And I am rejoicing in His goodness
And daily mercy that I see.

My Life

Lord, I am submitting my life
To your total care,
And I am thankful for your holy presence
That is ever so near.

Lord, I am submitting my life
To align with your will,
For my heart's desires and my destiny,
Only You can fulfill.

Lord, I am submitting my life
To the discipline of fasting and prayer,
For there are greater fruits for your kingdom
That I still need to bear.

I See God

I see God in the simple things
And in the bountiful blessings
That He daily brings.

I see God in the deep blue sea
As I ponder all that He has done for me.
I see God in the skies above
And the wonderful display of His perfect love.

I see God in my family and friends,
And I am thankful
For the warmth and hospitality
That they so cheerfully extend.

I Cannot Take

I cannot ever take any glory,
For God is the Author
And the Finisher of my story.

I cannot ever take any glory,
For it is only by His grace
That I am able to live holy.

I cannot ever take any glory,
So my reasonable service
Is to say thank You, Lord Jesus,
And worship Him only.

Lord Jesus

Lord Jesus, I magnify your Word,
And I thank You for bearing witness
Where ever it is heard.

Lord Jesus, I bow down at your feet,
And I thank You for the mercy seat.
Lord Jesus, I thank You
For Your precious blood
And the love that You have shown me
From heaven up above.

Lord I Am Thankful

Lord, I am thankful
That your Holy Spirit is always with me,
And He bears witness to the fact
That I am totally free.

Lord, I am thankful
That your Holy Spirit is always in me,
And He helps me to believe
What my eyes cannot see.

Lord, I am thankful
That your Holy Spirit is always upon
To empower me to carry out your master plan.

Lord, I am thankful
That your Holy Spirit is always for me,
And You are committed to complete
What You have started in me.

You Have

Lord, I am thankful
That You have calmed the storm
And that You are holding me
In your outstretched arms.

Lord, I am thankful
That You have calmed the storm,
And You have ministered your healing balm.

Lord, I am thankful
That You have calmed the storm,
And You have given me your grace to carry on.

I Am Taking Time

I am taking time to relax
And take control.
I am taking time to be kind
To my body and soul.

I am taking time to give thanks
For the air that I breathe.
I am taking time to give thanks
For I have all that I need.

When I Gazed

When I gazed into the eyes of Majesty,
I say, Lord, thank You for the things
That You have done for me.

I say thank You for dying upon the cross
To save a soul that was totally broken and lost.
I say thank You for my daily provision
And your host of angelic protection.

Lord, I say thank You for the knowledge
And wisdom that You give,
And for the Grace and the mercy
That You grant me to live.

Thank You

Lord, I thank You for the fresh air
That I am breathing today.
I thank You for your promise
That You will always make a way.

Lord, I thank You
For your holy presence,
That is always so near.
Lord, I thank You for blessing me
With the fruits of answered prayers.

There Is

There is a secret place
Where I can go,
Where the fountain of living water flows.

It is a place of peace and solitude
Where I lose every negative attitude.
It is a place of greater altitude,
Where I am compelled to express my true gratitude.

I Would Never

Lord, I would never make it in my own strength,
For on the arm of my flesh,
I can never depend.

Lord, I would never make it in my own strength,
For on the cares of this world,
All of my energy would be spent.

Lord, I would never make it in my own strength,
For every good and perfect gift
Comes only from the Father above,
Who daily nourishes and uplift.

Poems of Heartfelt Prayers

The effective fervent prayer of a righteous man avails much.
—James 5:16

I Am Looking

Lord, I am looking
Through your eyes of perfect love,
And I am drawing new strength
From heaven up above.

Lord, I am looking
Through your eyes of forgiveness,
And my sins and my weaknesses,
I do humbly confess.

Lord, I am looking
Through your eyes of mercy and truth,
And I am praying
That my life would make a difference
By bearing much fruits.

I Give You

Lord, I give You my painful memories
And all of my insecurities.
Lord, I give You the negative thoughts
That assails my mind
And the piercing arrows of every kind.

Lord, I give You each one of my unmet desires,
And I am asking for grace to accomplish
What my calling requires.

Lord, I give You every struggle
That is hidden in my soul,
For You know the true depth of my story
That has never been told.

I Am Willing, Lord

I am willing, Lord, to fast and pray,
For I am desperate to hear
What your Spirit has to say.

I am willing, Lord, to fast and pray,
And I am trusting You to lead me
And show me your way.

I am willing, Lord, to fast and pray,
For in this critical hour,
There is really no more time left to play.

Holy Spirit

Holy Spirit, come and lead the way,
And give me wisdom for today.
Holy Spirit, come and lead the way,
And teach me how and what to pray.

Holy Spirit, come and lead the way,
And let me hear what heaven has to say.
Holy Spirit, come and lead the way,
And from your side, never let me stray.

I Am Listening

Lord, I am listening for your still small voice
To tell me what to do.
Lord, I am listening for your still small voice,
To tell me where to go.

Lord, I am listening for your still small voice
To call me even closer to your side.
Lord, I am listening for your still small voice
To whisper words from heaven above
And teach me how to walk in your perfect love.

In View Of

Lord, help me to live my life
In view of eternity,
And let me endeavor to be all
That You have created me to be.

Lord, help me to live my life
In view of eternity,
And let me mentor the ones
That You have entrusted to me.

Lord, help me to live my life
In view of eternity,
Knowing that the face of my Savior,
Someday I will see.

Lord, help me to live my life
In view of eternity,
And let me be a vessel
That brings much honor and glory to You.

A Panoramic View

Lord, give me a panoramic view
Of the things that I see here on earth.
Lord, give me sound wisdom
To walk in the light
And help me to love You
And do what is right.

Lord, give me a panoramic view,
And to your holy calling,
Let me always be true.
Lord, give me a panoramic view,
And daily, give me the strength
That I need to get through.

Teach Me

Lord, teach me how
To come and abide,
And in your holy presence,
Help me daily to hide.

Lord, teach me how
To come and abide,
And never let me doubt You
Or stray from your side.

Lord, teach me how
To come and abide,
And let my time spend with You;
Be a very joyful ride.

Never Let Me

Lord, never let me waiver at your promises,
And never let me take for granted
The daily blessings that You give.

Lord, let me never grow weary in my daily walk,
And never let me stumble in the dark.
Lord, let me never fail to declare
That your Word is true,
And never let me muse over the challenges
Or the things that I have been through.

Let There Be

Lord, let there be prosperity within my gates,
And let me daily experience your abounding grace.
Lord, let your favor shine brightly upon my path
And help me daily to keep You in my thoughts.

Lord, fill my life with vitality,
And help me to walk in your victory.
Lord, give me a pure heart
That is surrendered to You,
And show me the things that You want me to do.

I Am Heeding

Lord, I am heeding your command
To watch and pray,
And I am asking You to lead me
And show me your way.

Lord, I am heeding your command
To watch and pray,
And I am listening daily to hear
What the Holy Spirit has to say.

Lord, I am heeding your command
To watch and pray,
For within your inner courts,
I am delighted to stay.

Let My Prayers

Father, let my prayers be a reflection
Of your heavenly desires,
And let them pierce through the clouds,
Like a flaming fire.

Father, let my prayers be a reflection
Of your heavenly desires
And satisfy the soul that is panting
To come on up higher.

Father, let my prayers be a reflection
Of your heavenly desires,
And give me a heart that is obedient
To do whatever you require.

Lift Up My Eyes

Lord, lift up my eyes
From the pain that I see,
And help me to walk in the path
That You have chosen for me.

Lord, lift up my eyes
From the pain that I see,
And help me to walk
Like a child that is totally free.

Lord, lift up my eyes
From the pain that I see,
And let my life be an example
Of a fruit bearing tree.

Override My Will

Heavenly Father, override my will
And let your divine purpose
In my life be fulfilled.

Heavenly Father, override my will
And command the trouble waters
In my life to be still.

Heavenly Father, override my will
As I lift up my eyes
And look to the hills.

Heavenly Father, override my will
And let me walk in your love
And experience no ill.

Root Out

Lord, root out every iniquity of old
And bring an abiding peace within my soul.
Lord, root out every iniquity of old
And bring deliverance
Where the enemy once had control.

Lord, root out every iniquity of old
And let me daily abide in the Shepherd's fold.
Lord, root out every iniquity of old
And fulfill my secret desires
That has never been told.

Lord, root out every iniquity of old
And light your holy fire in the place
Where my heart has grown cold.

Lord Give Me

Lord, give me the spirit of wisdom
And revelation in the knowledge of You,
And show me the things
That You want me to do.

Lord, give me the spirit of wisdom
And revelation in the knowledge of You,
And let me walk in the full redemption
That You have purchased for me.

Lord, give me the spirit of wisdom
And revelation in the knowledge of You,
And let my life be a holy offering
That is well pleasing to You.

Make Me a Sniper

Lord, make me a sniper
With your spoken Word,
And let it penetrate the darkness,
Wherever it is heard.

Lord, make me a sniper
With your spoken Word,
And let it go down deep
Into the fiber of the body and soul.

Lord, make me a sniper
With your spoken Word,
And teach me how
To master the two-edged sword.

Lord, make me a sniper
With your spoken Word,
And let it amplify, like a megaphone
That is coming directly from the Father's throne.

Lord Let

Lord, let there be an open heaven,
And multiply your blessings seventy times seven.
Lord, let us hear your lightning and thunder,
And let us see the true evidence
Of Your miracles, signs, and wonders.

Lord, let us see rivers of your glory,
And give us a fresh revelation of your gospel story.
Lord, let this be a season of restitution
And bring restoration out of devastation.
Lord, let this be a season of rest and refreshing,
And let our lives on this earth be a beautiful blessing.

Take Me Beyond

Lord, heal the barren areas in my life,
And let your Holy Spirit bring creativity,
For with You, there is no impossibility.

Lord, take me beyond what I am able to see
To the table that You have prepared for me.
Lord, let me see your resurrection power,
And let me be a witness for You
In this day and this hour.

Let

Lord, let the light of your glory
Shine brightly in me,
And let it destroy every darkness
That my eyes cannot see.

Lord, let your Word go down deep
And bear much fruit in me,
And let me walk in your power and authority.

Lord, let your love keep growing stronger
And stronger in me,
And help me to lavishly share it,
Knowing that You gave it for free.

Holy Spirit Teach Me

Holy Spirit, teach me who I am,
And grant me the grace
That I need to stand.

Holy Spirit, teach me who I am,
And help me to be faithfully obedient
To God's master plan.
Holy Spirit, teach me how to pray,
And keep me on the straight and narrow way.

Remove Every Iniquity

Lord, remove every iniquity from my family tree,
And open up the good book
To my divine destiny.

Lord, remove every iniquity from my family tree,
And let me worship and serve You
From a heart that is true.

Lord, remove every iniquity from my family tree,
And restore the years that were stolen
By giving me latter days that are prosperous and golden.

Lord, remove every iniquity from my family tree,
And bring a heavenly intervention
To change the course of my life and my current situation.

Heal the Trauma

Lord, heal the hidden trauma
That I have suffered in my soul,
And deliver my life
From any bondages of old.

Lord, heal the hidden places
Where sin still abounds,
And turn everything in my life around.

Lord, heal the many wounds
That I have painfully endured,
And multiply your blessings more and more.

Lord I Care

Lord, I care more for your kingdom
Than I do about earthly stuff.
And if you never do another thing for me,
You have already done more than enough.

Lord, You have chosen me
To be a part of your beautiful creation,
And You have adorned me with your love
And your free gift of salvation.

Lord, You have shown me your mercy,
And You have given me forgiveness.
Lord, You have been a tower of strength
In the moments of my weakness.

Give Me Your

Lord, give me your eyes to see
That beyond every life circumstance,
Nothing with You is by happenstance.

Lord, give me your vision,
Which is bigger than me;
And help me not to focus
On the things that I see.

Lord, give me your ears,
And help me to hear
The voice of the Good Shepherd,
Who is ever so near.

Lord, give me a heart
That is yielded to You,
And help me to be a servant
That is faithful and true.

The Fullness

Lord, open wide my spiritual eyes,
And help me to appreciate your love
And your selfless sacrifice.

Lord, open wide your heavenly gates,
And let me grasp your full provision
And receive it by faith.

Lord, open wide my spiritual ears,
And let me hear You in the Spirit
And exhibit no fear.

Lord Fill Me

Lord, fill me with your holy fire,
And let my heart burn daily with your desires.
Lord, place your Word upon my lips,
And let me always use it to uplift.
Lord, place your songs within my heart,
And from your side, never let me depart.

Your True Desires

Lord, put your true desires within my heart,
And occupy my mind and my innermost thoughts.
Lord, put your true desires within my heart,
And teach me how to listen and when I should talk.
Lord, put your true desires within my heart,
And from your righteous ways, let me never depart.

Lord Hide Me

Lord, hide me from the plots of the enemy,
And protect me from the evil
That I am not able to see.

Lord, hide me from any acts of willful sin
And the snares that the tempter tries to bring.
Lord hide me from my own selfishness,
And forgive me when I come to You and confess.

Lord, hide me from the spirit of discouragement,
And let your true joy become my daily strength.
Lord, hide me from every form of deception,
And let your Word be my mirror for reflection.

Let Me Move

Lord, let me move beyond theology
To a life of your perfect liberty.
Lord, let me move beyond what I can see
To the perfect plan that You have for me.
Lord, let me move beyond my comfort zone
And take my rightful position at the Father's throne.

Until You Come

Lord, help me to occupy until You come,
And anoint me for the race
That You have called me to run.

Lord, help me to occupy until You come,
And let me exercise my God-given authority
And walk in your resurrection power and victory.

I Am Stretching

Lord, I am stretching forth my hands in faith,
And I am coming to your throne without hesitate.
Lord, I am stretching forth my hands in faith,
And on every one of your promises,
I will daily meditate.

Lord, I am stretching forth my hands in faith,
And on your perfect timing and fulfillment,
I will continue to trust and patiently wait.

Do Not Let

Lord, do not let my faith become a mockery,
And don't let me experience the oppression of the enemy.
Lord, do not let my faith become a mockery
Since I dare to believe what my eyes cannot see.

Lord, do not let my faith become a mockery,
For Jesus's blood has paid the price for my victory.
Lord, do not let my faith become a mockery,
But let me walk as a child that is totally free.

Help Me to Follow

Lord, help me to follow your perfect plan,
And never let me rely on my own strength
Or the opinion of man.

Lord, help me to follow your perfect plan,
And remind me that You are holding me daily
In the palm of your hands.

Lord, help me to follow your perfect plan,
And help me to always trust your faithfulness,
Even when my mind cannot understand.

Hide Me

Lord, hide me in your secret place
And let me gaze upon your lovely face.
Lord, hide me in your secret place
And lavish me with your amazing grace.
Lord, hide me in your secret place
And give me courage to endure
In the course of my race.

Teach Me How

Holy Spirit, teach me how to follow your lead,
And at heavens banquet table,
Let me find everything that I need.

Holy Spirit, teach me how to follow your lead,
And for every command that You give me,
Give me a heart that is sensitive and ready to heed.

Let Me Experience

Lord, let me experience the reality
Of your written Word,
And let it settle every issue
That I have seen and heard.

Lord, let me experience the reality
Of your written Word,
And satisfy my longing
For the things that I yearn.

Lord, let me experience the reality
Of your written Word,
And let me walk in your favor
On the face of this earth.

Lord Free Me

Lord, free me from the limitations
That are hindering me,
And lift up my spiritual eyes to see.

Lord, free me from the limitations
That are hindering me,
And empower me to be the woman
That You have created me to be.

Lord, free me from the limitations
That are hindering me,
And let me walk in the pathway
That You have chosen for me.

When I Am

Lord, when I am feeling weak,
Please make me strong.
And when I am persecuted for doing right,
Help me to keep on walking in the light.

Lord, when I am feeling weak,
Please make me strong.
And help me to keep trusting in your perfect plan.

Lord, when I am feeling weak,
Please make me strong.
And teach me how to listen
And follow your command.

Search My Heart

Lord Jesus, search my heart today,
And teach me what I need to pray.
Lord Jesus, search my heart today,
And grant me wisdom on life's way.
Lord Jesus, search my heart today,
And keep my feet from going astray.

Dying Daily

Lord, I am dying daily
To the desires of my flesh,
And I am trusting in your goodness,
And I am learning not to fret.

Lord, I am dying daily
To the desires of my flesh,
And by the blood of the Lamb,
I am overcoming every test.

Lord, I am dying daily
To the desires of my flesh,
And in the finished work of my Savior,
I will patiently rest.

Let My Life

Lord, let my life be an expression
Of your love here on earth
And bring restoration to me and my family
As a result of the new birth.

Lord, let my life be an expression
Of your love here on earth
And bring healing and anointing
To every area where I hurt.

Lord, let my life be an expression
Of your love here on earth
And teach me how to follow You
And stay spiritually alert.

Cleanse My Soul

Lord, cleanse my soul from every sin,
And give me peace and joy within.
Lord, cleanse my soul from every sin,
And deliver me from the snare
That the enemy brings.
Lord, cleanse my soul from every sin,
And to your holy Word and your presence,
Help me daily to cling.

Let Your Fire

Lord, let your holy fire fall today,
And help me as I kneel to pray.
Lord, let your holy fire fall today,
And on your perfect path,
Help me to daily stay.
Lord, let your holy fire fall today
And burn up every evil thing
That is standing in my way.

Turn Up the Volume

Lord, turn up the volume
Of your voice here on earth,
And let it resonate across the universe.

Lord, turn up the volume
Of your voice here on earth,
And take the hammer that is in your hand
And crush every evil deed that is known to man.

Open Up My Eyes

Lord, open up my eyes
To the truth of your Word,
And let me reject man's opinion
And the lies that I have heard.

Lord, open up my eyes,
To the truth of your Word,
And show me my true purpose
On the face of this earth.

Lord, open up my eyes
To the truth of your Word,
And remove every heavy burden
That has left me feeling weak and heavy laden.

Help Me

Help me, Lord, to do my part,
And strengthen me daily within my heart.
Help me, Lord, to do my part,
And teach me how
To cast down every idle thought.

Help me, Lord, to do my part,
And grant me your grace
When I have fallen so short.

Help me, Lord, to do my part,
And give me grace to persevere
And complete every task.

Open Up

Lord, open up my spiritual eyes to see
The heavenly vision that You have for me.
Lord, open up my spiritual eyes to see,
And let me partake in the inheritance
That You have laid out for me.
Lord, open up my spiritual eyes to see,
And let me blossom and flourish,
Like a fruitful tree.

The Efficacy

Lord, let the efficacy of your blood
Come and tear down everything
That is man made of.

Lord, let the efficacy of your blood
Flow freely in my life like a mighty flood.
Lord, let the efficacy of your blood
Come and reveal the true nature
Of what my life is made of.

A Fresh Refilling

Lord, give me a fresh refilling of the Holy Ghost,
And teach me the things
That I need to know most.
Lord, give me a fresh refilling of the Holy Ghost,
And satisfy my hunger for the things that I thirst.
Lord, give me a fresh refilling of the Holy Ghost,
And never let me grow weary or abandon my post.

Let Me See

Lord, open wide my spiritual eyes,
And let me see the true plan
That You have for my life.

Lord, open wide my spiritual eyes,
And help me to walk as a women of valor
That brings to your kingdom much glory and honor.

Lord, open wide my spiritual ears,
And let me know that in due time,
You will faithfully answer every prayer.

Let Me

Lord, let your Word grow down deep
Like a palm tree in me,
And let me move like the wind
That is totally free.

Lord, let my spirit grow strong,
Like the cedar of Lebanon,
And let my lips give You praise
For the things You have done.

Let my feet be planted firmly
In the house of the Lord,
And on the integrity of your Word,
Let me daily hold fast.

Lord, let me bring forth much fruit
In my latter days,
And help me to live pure and holy
In all of my ways.

Father Help Me

Father, help me to be committed
To your heavenly call,
And help me to serve You
And give You my all.

Father, help me to find your solutions
To the problems of life,
And after the vain things of this world,
Help me never to strive.

Father, help me to always confess
That your Word is true,
And help me daily to keep my eyes upon You.

Keep My Heart

Lord, keep my heart from deception,
And help me to walk in your direction.
Lord, keep my heart from deception,
And help me to be open to your correction.

Lord, keep my heart from deception,
And let your Word be my daily mirror of reflection.
Lord, keep my heart from deception,
And help me to live in your love and perfection.

Help Me to Walk

Lord, help me to walk daily
In your perfect light,
And grant me your grace
To do what is right.

Lord, help me to walk daily
In your perfect light,
And let the reflection from your mirror
Shine ever so bright.

Lord, help me to walk daily
In your perfect light,
And help me to contend for the faith
And stand strong in the fight.

Give Me

Lord, give me sound wisdom
To know what to do,
And grant me the grace that is needed
To carry it through.

Lord, give me sound wisdom
To know what to do,
And help me daily by your Spirit
To trust only in You.

Lord, give me sound wisdom
To act on my faith,
And grant me your patience
When You know I should wait.

I Am Willing

Lord, I am willing to make the changes
To accomplish your will.
So for more of your anointing,
Give me a daily refill.

Lord, I am willing to make the changes
To accomplish your will.
And beside the quiet waters, I long to be still.

Lord, I am willing to make the changes
To accomplish your will.
So I am surrendering everything in my attitude
That I know I should kill.

An Emptiness

Lord, there is an emptiness
That only You can fill,
So I am offering up my empty cup
And I am asking You to fill it up.

Lord, there is an emptiness
That only You can fill,
For my true strength and my courage
Comes only from the hill.

Lord, there is an emptiness
That only You can fill,
So please speak to my soul
And command it to be still.

Holy Fire

Lord, let your holy fire burn in me
And help me to fulfill my divine destiny.
Lord, let your holy fire burn in me
And open wide my spiritual eyes to see.

Lord, let your holy fire burn in me
And unlock every door that is a mystery.
Lord, let your holy fire burn in me,
And let me birth forth every desire
That You have placed within me.

Lord Fill My Cup

Lord, fill my cup to overflow
And let your Spirit rest upon me
Where ever I may go.

Lord, fill my cup to overflow,
And in your love and kindness,
Help me daily to grow.

Lord, fill my cup to overflow,
And with much joy and laughter,
Let my countenance glow.

Lord I Am Asking

Lord, I am asking You
To fulfill my divine destiny,
For only You know the true person
That You have created me to be.

Lord, I am asking You
To fulfill my divine destiny,
By unlocking the hidden treasures
That You have placed inside of me.

Lord, I am asking You
To fulfill my divine destiny
And help me not to focus
On the negative things that I see.

Eye to Eye

Lord, You have said
That I would see you eye to eye,
And that my sons and my daughters would prophesy.

Lord, You have said
That I would see You eye to eye,
And that on the integrity of your Word, I can daily rely.

Lord, You have said
That I will see You eye to eye,
And that every desire of my heart, You will satisfy.

Lord Help Me to Rest

Lord, help me to rest
In the finished work
That You did upon Calvary.

Lord, help me to rest
In the finished work,
And help me to fulfill my divine destiny.

Lord, help me to find favor
In all of my labor,
And let me live the abundant life
That was purchased by my wonderful Savior.

Help Me to Forget

Lord, help me to forget
The pain of my youth,
And help me daily to walk
In your perfect truth.

Lord, help me to forget
The things that are dead,
And help me to walk
In your resurrection power instead.

I Am Not

Lord, I am not seeking your face
For mere silver and gold,
But I am seeking for the mystery
Of my life to unfold.

Lord, I am not seeking your face
For just spiritual gifts,
But I am seeking for an answer
That would cause other's burdens to lift.

Lord, I am not seeking your face
To be seen by the crowd,
But when You speak,
I want to know that I am hearing You clear and loud.

A Fresh Dose

Lord, give me a fresh dose
Of your holy fire,
And burn up every vain
And ungodly desire.
Lord, give me a fresh dose
Of your holy fire,
And help me to accomplish
What my calling require.

Occupy Every Room

Lord, I am asking You
To occupy every room in my heart,
And from the path of your righteousness,
Let me never depart.

Lord, I am asking You
To occupy every room in my heart.
And shine the light of your Word
On everything that is dark.

Lord, I am asking You
To occupy every room in my heart,
And help me to bring discipline to my flesh
And my innermost thoughts.

Let Me Regain

Lord, help me to regain every ground
That I have lost in the fight,
And let me experience my full redemption
And walk in the light.

Lord, help me to regain every ground
That I have lost in the fight,
And help me to live a life of victory
In the power of your might.

Lord Let Me

Lord, let me follow your leading,
One step at a time,
And let your kingdom connections
Fully come into line.

Lord, let me echo here on earth
What I am hearing from heaven,
And let love be the ingredient
That I am spreading like leaven.

Lord, let my life be a light
Where the darkness exist,
And when I encounter any evil,
Give me your power to resist.

My Position

Lord, teach me how to maintain,
My position in prayer,
And when I call upon your name,
Let your holy presence be near.

Lord, teach me how to maintain
My position in prayer,
And let me humbly receive every instruction
That You are wanting me to hear.

Lord, teach me how to maintain
My position in prayer,
And let me receive every promise
That I have been claiming through the years.

Lord Remove

Lord, remove every form of hindrance,
And let my life on this earth make a difference.
Lord, remove every form of hindrance,
And let me walk in my true deliverance.

Lord, remove every form of hindrance,
And keep me from presumption and ignorance.
Lord, remove every form of hindrance,
And give me the opportunity of a second chance.

Lord Unlock

Lord, unlock your Spirit of creativity,
And let it manifest in my life
And bring honor and glory to You.

Lord, unlock your Spirit of creativity,
And let your daughter shine like the star
That You have created her to be.

Lord When

Lord, when I fail to hear
Your still small voice,
Come and open wide my spiritual ears.

Lord, when obstacles are standing in my way,
Please let me hear clearly
What the Holy Spirit has to say.

Lord, when my mind cannot seem to understand,
Please show me your blueprint
And help me to carry out your master plan.

Let The Heavens

Lord, let the heavens thunder,
When I call out your name;
And let your glory penetrate,
Every fiber of my frame.

Lord, let the heavens thunder,
When I call out your name;
And let me abide daily in your presence,
And never be the same.

Lord Hear Me

Lord, hear me when I call your name,
And to your kingdom, let me bring no shame.
Lord, let my eyes be fixed on You,
And let each prayer of mine come true.

Lord, bring me to that place of peace,
With a servants heart to obey and please.
Lord, give me a fresh vision of your love
And multiply your anointing from heaven above.

Order My Feet

Lord, order my feet,
One step at a time,
And keep me from falling
Or stepping out of line.

Lord, order my feet
On the path that is ahead.
And help me to yield to your Spirit
And never to the dictates of my head.

Lord Sometimes

Lord, sometimes I wonder where You are
And why your holy presence often seems so far.
Lord, sometimes I wonder where You are
And why my soul is still wrestling
With some wounded scars.
Lord, sometimes I wonder where You are
When I am feeling tired and weary
From fighting in this spiritual war.

Lord Awaken

Lord, awaken my spirit
To that much higher call.
And let me run with endurance
And give You my all.

Lord, awaken my spirit
To hear the voice of the King,
And a true heart of worship,
Help me daily to bring.

Lord, awaken my spirit
To your joy that's within.
And help me to give thanks
That You are getting ready
To do a brand new thing.

Lord Help Me

Lord, help me to reach this generation
With the gospel of salvation.
Help me to move beyond mediocrity
And man's opinion and theology.

Lord, help me to move beyond complacency,
To combat the present evils that I see.
Lord, help me to move beyond the confusion,
To seek for your wisdom and solution.

Let There

Lord, let there be a hundredfold return
On the good seeds that I have sown.
And let there be a double recompense
For the painful things that I have known.

Lord, let there be a supernatural grace
To continue in my race.
And let the light of your glory be seen upon my face.

I Am Crying

Lord, I am crying because my words are too inadequate
To aptly describe how I feel.
I am crying because my heart cannot understand
The pain and the suffering that I have seen in this land.
Lord, I am crying for the eyes that are too blind to see
And the ears that are too dull to hear.

Lord, I am crying for the hearts that are harden by life
And the ones who are daily struggling just to survive.
Lord, I am crying for the future generation
That is staring back at us,
Wondering who in this world can they possibly trust.

Your Living Water

Lord, let your living water flow,
And let fruits abound wherever I go.
Lord, revive me with your holy fire,
And fill my heart with your desires.

Lord, answer me swiftly when I call,
And anchor my feet so I will not fall.
Lord, come and deliver this prisoner of hope,
For there is no earthly problem
That is beyond your scope.

I Am Praying

Lord, I am praying to experience You
In a much deeper way,
And I am listening to hear
What the Holy Spirit has to say.

Lord, I am praying for the eyes
Of every nation to see
And for everyone that is held captive,
To be totally set free.

Lord, I am praying for the ones
Who are broken in their hearts,
And I am asking for mercy
For the lives that are so torn apart.

Recompense

Lord, I am asking You for recompense,
For You are my one and only strong defense.
Lord, I am asking You for recompense
And a renewing of my inner strength.

Lord, I am asking You for recompense
And a sharpening of my spiritual lens.
Lord, I am asking You for recompense
For every evil thing that has ever been sent.

I Don't Want

Lord, I don't want anything
That will cause me to stress,
And I don't want anything
That You cannot bless.

Lord, I don't want anything
That is only temporary,
And I don't want anything
That I can get in a hurry.

Lord, I don't want anything
That is gotten by selfish gain,
And I don't ever want anything
That would cause You any pain.

Prepare My Heart

Lord, prepare my heart to receive your Word,
And let the incorruptible seed produce a harvest
In the soil where it is sown.

Lord, prepare my heart to receive your Word,
And never let it be uprooted
By the cares of this world.

I Am Trusting

I am trusting in a God
That I cannot see,
But daily to His throne room,
I am making my plea.

I am trusting in a God
That I cannot see,
But I believe that He hears,
And He is answering me.

I am trusting in a God
That I cannot see,
But I know that He has fashioned my frame,
And He truly cares about me.

An Unshakeable Consecration

Lord, let me have an unshakeable consecration,
And give me a true heart of appreciation
For the people of your creation.

Lord, let me have an unshakeable consecration,
And give me supernatural insight
Into the plight of this present generation.

Lord, let me have an unshakeable consecration,
And give me greater understanding and revelation.
Lord, let me have an unshakeable consecration,
And let me meet daily at your filling station.

I Am Crying Out

Lord, I am crying out
To see the fruits of answered prayers,
For You have said that when I call,
You will immediately hear.

Lord, I am crying out
To see the fruits of answered prayers
And a greater sense that your presence
Is ever so near.

Lord, I am crying out
For your Word to become more real to me.
Lord, I am crying out
For my spiritual eyes to see.

Lord, I am crying out
To see the fruits of answered prayers
Because the anguish in my soul
Is just too hard to bear.

Lord, I am crying out
To see the fruits of answered prayers
And a healing from the effects
Of life's wear and tear.

Prayers of Encouragement/ Comfort/Condolence

Therefore comfort each other and edify one
another, just as you also are doing.
—1 Thessalonians 5:11

A Genuine Gem

You are a genuine gem,
And there is only one of you.
So keep on shining wherever you go,
And you will reap a great harvest
In the lives where you sow.

Keep on shining your light,
For you are a gift to the world.
And remember to live by the conviction
That is deep down in your soul.

I Pray

I pray that God will remove
Every pain and residue from your past
And give you joy unspeakable that will last.
May he restore your true sense of identity
And help you to walk in total victory.

I pray that God will heal the trauma
That your soul has endured
And give you the greater treasures
That He has laid up in store.

Never Alone

You are never alone
In your darkest hour,
For God is your light
And the source of all power.

You are never alone
When you are facing the storm,
For God is your strength
Through the breaking of dawn.

You are never alone
If your heart remains true,
For the Author and Finisher
Will always carry you through.

Lift Up Your Hands

Lift up your hands
And turn up the praise,
For God wants to refine you
And reset your pace.

Lift up your hands
And turn up the praise,
For this is no time to grow weary,
And no time to waste.

Lift up your hands
And turn up the praise,
For God wants to reset you
And ignite your faith.

You Don't

You don't have to receive
Every negative thought
That flies into your mind.
For they will only lead to bondage
And control you in time.

You don't have to believe
Everything that you see with your eyes,
But know the real difference
Between the truth and a lie.

You don't have to react
To everything that you feel,
But choose to act on God's Word
And continue to kneel.

Hope

Hope is an anchor in my soul,
For I am a child of the King
And a sheep in His fold.

Hope gives me mercy for each new day
And helps me on the path
When I need to pray.

Hope gives me the patience
When I need to wait.
Hope helps me to receive
When I have acted on my faith.

I Am Free

I am free to be a child
Of the Most High God.
I am free to honor and worship Him
With everything that I have.

I am free to be a child
Of the Most High God.
I am free to receive comfort
From His staff and rod.

I am free to be a child
Of the Most High God.
I am free to daily love and serve Him,
Whether I am happy or I am feeling sad.

Everybody

Everybody needs a little treasure box
Filled with faith, hope, and love
That is given from above.

Everybody needs a little quiet time
To pause and practice self-care
And just simply unwind.

Faith

Faith is not a feeling
Or the direction that your mind is leading.
Faith is not an affiliation
Or a certain denomination.

Faith is about trusting in your Creator—
The all-knowing One who is greater.
Faith is believing who He says He is
And receiving the free gift of salvation
That His only begotten Son, Jesus, came to give.

If You Want

If you want to find joy
That will eternally last,
You have to look at Jesus
And not the images of your past.

If you want to find the living water
That will quench every thirst,
You have to take a fresh drink
From the fountain of the Holy Ghost.

Your Strength

Your strength can't be found
In the philosophy of man.
Your strength can't be found
In the things that you hold.

Your strength can't be found
In the people that you know,
For it is only God's grace and wisdom
That can help you to grow.

A Little Sparkle

Leave a little sparkle
On your pathway each day.
Try adding a little kindness
To the things that you say.

Leave a little sparkle
On your pathway each day,
And remember to be thankful,
And take time out to pray.

Beyond Your Pain

Beyond your pain,
There is a bountiful gain.
Beyond your disappointments,
God has a new appointment.

Beyond your deepest struggles,
There is a double blessing for your troubles.
Beyond your fears,
There is joy for your tears.
And beyond man's rejection,
There is God's unconditional love
And His divine protection.

Lord You Are

Lord, You are my sunshine
On a cloudy day.
You are the perfect lamp
That lights my way.

Lord, You are the morning star
That shines so bright.
You are the One
Who turns every wrong to right.

Lord, You are the anchor
That I steadfast hold.
You are the Good Shepherd
And the gatekeeper of my soul.

Wisdom

Wisdom is far better
Than silver and gold.
Wisdom is far better
Than the things that you hold.

Wisdom will give you success
In all of your ways.
Wisdom will add laughter
To the length of your days.

Wisdom will lead you
On the path that is straight.
Wisdom will teach you to have patience
And show you how to wait.

Wisdom will bless you
And keep your life youthful.
Wisdom will add years
And make your life fruitful.

In The Path

Lord, for those who are caught
In the path of the storm,
I pray for Your angelic assistance
To bring them peace and calm.

Lord, for those who are homeless
And left without hope,
I pray that You would provide shelter
And show them how to cope.

Lord, for those who feel helpless
With no sign of where to turn,
I pray that they will find grace and mercy
By coming to your throne.

Never Say

Never say that you are too busy
To take the time to pray.
Never say that you are too busy
For the King of kings today.

Never say that you are too busy
To take the time to sing,
For every activity of daily living
Should begin and end with Him.

When You Are

When you are feeling lonely in the fight,
You can be strong in the power of His might.
When you are feeling like you can't go on,
You can reach out and take His outstretched arms.

When you are uncertain of what choice to make,
His divine wisdom will show you
Which pathway you should take.
When the road that is ahead seems difficult,
Ask God to give you the grace
That you need to walk it out.

God's Word

The grass will surely wither,
And the flowers will certainly fade.
But God's Word will stand forever,
And Jesus's blood will be your daily cover.

The grass will surely wither,
And the flowers will certainly fade.
But God's Word is alive and powerful,
And it will overcome everything that is harmful.

Old Pharaoh

Old Pharaoh will tell you
That you will never be free.
But don't listen to his lies,
And don't you agree.

Old Pharaoh will entice you
To return to your mess,
But just look to your Savior
And you will pass every test.

Old Pharaoh will remind you
Of the onions and of leeks.
And He will threaten
That if you ever leave him,
You will have nothing left to eat.

But Jesus owns the cattle on a thousand hills,
And every one of His promises,
He will faithfully fulfill.

Be Kind

Be kind to other people
When you are on your way up.
Never cause a brother or sister to stumble,
But always endeavor to stay gentle and humble.

Be kind with the words
That comes out of your mouth.
For people are dealing daily
With their own fears and doubts.

Be kind to the people
Who are feeling sad and down.
And share a little laughter
That will turn around their frown.

Take Time

Take time to laugh;
Take time to play.
Take time to show a little kindness
On your pathway each day.

Take time to rest,
And say no to stress.
Take time to be authentic,
And always do your very best.

Note

There are not enough words
To give you thanks
For the kindness that you have shown to me.

There are not enough words
To fill up the page
Of this note that I am sending to you.

Thank you!

Stop

Stop living your life
At the mercy of man.
And stop stressing over things
That you cannot understand.

Stop living your life
At the mercy of man.
But daily seek for God's wisdom,
And do what you can.

Stop living your life
At the mercy of man.
But seek for the true favor
That comes only from God's hands.

I Write

I write from my heart
And not from my head,
For someone might need a kind word
For the road that is ahead.

I write about the pain
And the injustices that I see,
For my inner soul is always crying.
Lord Jesus, please set every prisoner free!

Faithfulness

You can always depend upon God's faithfulness
To give you victory over every test.
You can always depend upon the Comforter
To speak peace to your heart like no other.

You can always depend upon God's holy Word,
For He will manifest His glory
Wherever it is heard.

Calm the Storm

Lord, I am asking You
To calm the storm,
And administer your healing balm.

Lord, I am asking You
To calm the storm,
And give me the courage to carry on.

Lord, I am asking You
To calm the storm,
And keep me from all pain and harm.

I Have To

I have to be real;
I have to be free.
I have to be all
That God created me to be.

I have to be real;
I have to be free.
For I am a very precious pearl,
And there is only one of me.

Jesus Is Risen

Clothe yourself with humility,
And wake up to the sound of victory.
Wake up to His resurrection power,
And honor the King
In this day and this hour.

Wake up with hope
And a new attitude,
For your Savior is risen,
And that is the real truth.

Never

Never buy the lies
That the enemy sells,
But wake up to God's Word,
And declare it is well.

Never eat from the tree
That is bearing bad fruits,
But put your trust in Jesus,
And keep walking in the truth.

Today

Today I am turning down my plate for you,
And I am asking the Lord for His healing balm
To anoint your body and drive back the storm.

Today I am turning down my plate for you,
And I am asking God for His amazing grace
To anchor your soul in His secret place.
Today I am turning down my plate for you,
For I am persuaded that the Word of God is true.

A Vision

When Jehovah places a vision
In the depth of your heart,
You must be willing to ask,
Lord, where should I start?

When Jehovah places a vision
In the depth of your heart,
You must trust Him to help you
To accomplish your part.

When Jehovah places a vision
In the depth of your heart,
You must believe that every enemy,
He has already fought.

When Jehovah places a vision
In the depth of your heart,
You must hold fast to your confession,
And never let the dream depart.

I Am Asking God

I am asking God
To give you peace within your soul
And draw you nearer to His fold.

I am asking God
To grant you grace for each new day
And lead you safely on life's way.

I am asking God
To grant you wisdom when you call
And fill you with His oil of joy.

I Am Praying

I am praying for God's mighty power
To daily transcend your soul
And deliver you from the pain of old.

I am praying for the presence of the Holy Ghost
To fill you with what you need most.
I am praying for God to bless you
In your latter years
And give you a double anointing for all of your tears.

Let Faith

Let faith get you up
When you are feeling down.
Let faith take your frown
And turn it around.

Let faith keep you believing
In the victory,
For faith has a substance
That your eyes cannot see.

Wisdom Says

Wisdom says to not put your trust
In the things of this world,
For some things can't be purchased
With silver and gold.

Wisdom says to not put your trust
In the philosophy of man,
For it is only the true Rock
That can help you to stand.

Wisdom says to not put your trust
In your own intellect,
For it will only inflate your ego
And lead you down the destructive path of regret.

Only God

It is good to have people
Who can tell you that they understand,
But it is only God
Who can reveal His true master plan.

It is good to have people
Who can lend you a helping hand,
But it is only God
Who can give you the grace that you need to stand.

It is good to have people
Who can counsel you,
But it is only God in His infinite wisdom
Who can daily show you what you need to do.

When

When I look over your life
And the things that have happened,
God has proven one thing—
That you have not been forgotten.

When others sent a message
To say that you were nothing,
God drew you to himself
And said, "I created you for something."

When your pain was much deeper
Than what words could express,
God reached out and touched you
And gave you His sweet rest.

Diversity

When we embrace one another's diversity,
We see a beautiful piece of God's tapestry.
When we treasure the gifts
That are found in each one,
They will encourage and unite us
To keep standing strong.
When we value each other's diversity,
We are really working for the good of humanity.

So Many

There are so many places
That I want to fly,
But I do not have the wings of a butterfly.

There are so many treasures
That I want to find.
Dear Lord, will You help me
To redeem the time?

There are so many dreams
That I want to fulfill.
Because there is a little girl in me
That wants to skip and run free.

You Can

You can be an instrument of change
In this day and this hour.
So tap into God's grace
And the strength of His power.

You can be an instrument of change
In this day and this hour,
And there are many hidden treasures
That only you can discover.

You can be an instrument of change
In this day and this hour,
For God is ready to stand by your side,
Like a mighty tower.

Oil of Joy

May the oil of joy keep on flowing
In the direction where you are going.
May the oil of joy keep on flowing,
And may your countenance keep on glowing.
May the oil of joy always refresh you,
And may the good Lord continue to bless you.

For Everyone

For everyone who said a prayer,
I thank you for your loving care.
For everyone who sent a gift,
Your love and your kindness did uplift.

To everyone who gave a hug,
In our hearts, we felt such a joyful tug.
And for everyone who shared their fond memories,
It was a testimony of our loved one's true faith and a
legacy!

Shine

Shine like the star
Wherever you go,
And be that beacon of light
That causes others to glow.

Shine like the star,
And be who you are.
For with your great gifts and personality,
You are bound to go far.

It Takes Faith

It takes faith to keep standing
When your head wants to quit.
It takes faith to keep going
When you don't seem to fit.

It takes faith to keep talking
When you are running out of words.
It takes faith to trust God
Over the negative things you have heard.

It takes faith to rejoice
When you are facing the storm.
It takes faith to believe God
When you doubt that He is leading you on.

Choose

Choose not to drown
In the middle of your pain,
But look for the sunshine
That comes after the rain.

Choose not to drown
In the middle of your pain,
For in that dungeon of darkness,
There is really no gain.

Spiritual Fruits

Use love as your key,
And joy as your gift.
Let peace be your guide,
And keep patience at your side.

Let kindness take you deeper
And God's favor will take you higher.
Let faithfulness mature you,
And let gentleness calm and adorn you.

But above all,
Let the spirit of self-control assist you
And keep you from the evil
That comes daily from the devil.

If The Enemy

If the enemy can persuade you
To give up your legal rights,
You will ignorantly surrender
In the middle of the fight.

If the enemy can persuade you
That God's Word cannot be true,
He will pervert those precious promises
And try to sell you something new.

If the enemy can persuade you
To give up your legal rights,
He will break in on your destiny,
Like a thief does in the night.

God Knows

God knows of the innermost pain
That you daily feel,
And He hears your heart cry
Every time that you kneel.

God sees every teardrop
That you have ever shed,
And He knows every thought
That your heart may have dread.

God knows every restless night
That you have ever spent,
And He will repay you for every heartache
That you have ever been dealt.

Lord Give Comfort

Lord, give comfort to the hurting hearts
Who are feeling pain and are torn apart.
Lord, let the balm of Gilead
Be the greatest comfort
That they have ever had.

Lord, help them to keep their eyes on You,
And show them daily what they need to do.
Lord, teach them how to find their way,
And grant them wisdom for each day.

Lord, help them not to feel alone,
But within their hearts,
Please come and make your home.
Lord, give them friends who will lift them up,
And grant them new mercy from heaven above.

May the Lord

May the Lord cause the light of His countenance
To shine brightly upon you
And give you grace for the task
That He has called you to do.

May the Lord cause the light of His countenance
To shine brightly upon you
And give you a divine strategy to navigate you through.

May the Lord cause the light of His countenance
To shine brightly upon you
And cause everything in this life
To work in favor for you.

Get Well

This get well wish has come to say
That a speedy recovery is on the way.
This get well wish has come to say
That I am available to help you in any way.
This get well wish has come to say
That I have mentioned your name in my prayers today.

Do Not

Do not ask God to turn back the tide,
For it will safely take you forth.
Do not seek to understand the why,
But humbly to His throne, draw nigh.

Do not cast away your confidence,
But trust God to be your strong defense.
Do not be led by what you see and feel,
But know that every broken piece,
In His mercy, God will surely heal.

Queen Esther

Queen Esther stood within the inner court
To request an audience with the King.
The King held out his golden scepter,
And Queen Esther touched the very tip.

The King asked Queen Esther, "What do you wish?
I will grant you your request."
So Queen Esther said, "If I have found favor in your sight,
Please save my people by the power of your might."

And the King could find no inner rest
Until he totally delivered Queen Esther's people
From a life of slavery and distress.

My Head

My head will never hang down low
Because of the faithfulness of Jehovah
That I have come to know.

My head will never hang down low,
For God has given me His precious promises,
And I truly believe that I am His.

My head will never hang down low,
For the Holy Spirit is teaching me
Everything in this life that I need to know.

Deborah Arose

Deborah arose as a mother
In the house of Israel,
And she was the commander of the army
When Sisera fell.

Deborah arose as a mother
In the house of Israel,
And while others relied upon horses and chariots,
She said, "In the name of Jehovah,
I am putting my trust."

Deborah arose as a mother
In the house of Israel,
And she used her God-given influence
To silence the threats of the enemy
And lead God's people into total victory.

We Are Sisters

We are sisters fellowshipping with other sisters,
And our voices are no silent whisper.
We are sisters daily demonstrating God's goodness,
And we are gentle vessels of His mercy and kindness.

We are sisters capturing life's precious moments,
And we are being transformed
In His likeness and wholeness.

We are sisters with God's heart and compassion,
And we are wearing love as a permanent fashion.
We are true sisters on a heavenly mission,
And we are fulfilling the great commission.

It Is Only God

It is only God who knows
The true heart of a man;
It is only He who can shed light
On what we cannot understand.

It is only God who knows
The path that is still ahead,
For in His eyes, every page of history
Has already been read.

It is only God who can grace us
With the ability to cope;
It is only His Word
That can give us a real reason to have hope.

Your Life

Stop living your life
Through other people's lens,
For the image that you see
Will never make any sense.

Stop wasting your life
Chasing after silver and gold,
For it can never buy you happiness,
And it cannot save your soul.

Stop living your life
With the ghost of your past.
It is time to reach out to your Creator,
And come out from the dark.

Poems of Faith/ Confession/Victory

Evening and morning and at noon I will pray, and
cry aloud, And He shall hear my voice.
—Psalms 55:17

I Am a General

I am a general in God's army,
And nothing evil will ever harm me.
I am a general in God's army,
And I am wearing His robe of righteousness.

I am a general in God's army,
And I am wearing His belt of truth.
I am a general in God's army,
And for His kingdom,
I am bearing much fruits.

I am a general in God's army,
And with my praise and worship,
I am daily making my moves.

I am a general in God's army,
And His helmet is protecting my mind.
I am a general in God's army,
And His peace is abiding in me.

I am a general in God's army,
And I am lifting up the shield of faith.
I am a general in God's army,
And the Holy Spirit is always near me.

My Soul

My soul finds victory in Elohim,
For there is no power on this earth
That is greater than Him.

My soul finds peace in Jehovah Shalom,
For there is a witness in my spirit
That I am truly His own.

My soul finds rest in Jesus's finished work,
For there is a joy that He keeps giving
To this prisoner of hope.

Jesus You Are

Jesus You are my Rock,
And not a stumbling block.
Jesus You are a friend
On who I can always depend.

Jesus, You are the anchor
That I steadfast hold.
Jesus, You are the healer
Of my body and soul.

Jesus, You are the source
From which all blessings descend.
Jesus, You are the true King
That is coming again.

I Do Not

I do not follow any religion
Or any man-made tradition.
I am just walking daily with Jesus
And fulfilling the great commission.

I do not need any accolades
Or any earthly position;
I only need God's wisdom in my every decision.

I do not need the approval
Or the opinion of man;
I only need to live by God's grace
And daily carry out His master plan.

It Is Time

It is time to burn up the bridges behind,
For there are many hidden treasures
That God wants me to find.

It is time to step out of the painful past
And move forward with courage
And a conviction of heart.

It is time to be obedient
To the heavenly call;
It is time to take hold of God's anchor
And know that I will not fall.

Jesus Is

Jesus is the fresh breath
That I daily take.
He is the new mercy that greets me
Every morning when I wake.

Jesus is the light
That shines brightly in the dark.
Jesus is the sunshine
That I daily meet upon my path.

Jesus is the sweetness
That fills my morning cup;
Jesus is the true joy
That daily perks me up.

The Only Ghost

The only ghost that I am entertaining
Is the power of the Holy Ghost.
The only costume that I am wearing
Is the true garment of praise.

The only treat that I am expecting
Is the abundance of amazing grace
And God's goodness and mercy
That will follow me for the rest of my days.

I Am Stepping Out

I am stepping out of my comfort zone
To a much deeper level
Than I have ever known.

I am stepping out of my insecurities
To discover new possibilities.
I am stepping out of the painful past
To make new friends and fond memories
That are sure to last.

Jesus Got Up

Jesus got up
So I don't have to stay down.
And whatever circumstances I am facing,
He is turning it around.

Jesus got up
So I don't have to stay down.
And He has risen up victoriously
And secured for me a heavenly crown.

Under the Blood

Under the blood of Jesus,
I am safe and secure.
Under the blood of Jesus,
I have cast every care.

Under the blood of Jesus,
I have perfect peace.
Under the blood of Jesus,
I have victory over sickness and disease.

I Submit

I submit to the Lordship of Jesus Christ,
And I offer up my body as a living sacrifice.
I submit to the blood and its cleansing power
To preserve and protect me in this critical hour.

I submit to the Name
Who is exalted on high,
For He has the power and the authority
That no one can ever deny.

I Refuse To

I refuse to take counsel
From fear and doubt,
For I am trusting that Jehovah
Will work everything out.

I refuse to take counsel
From fear and doubt,
But I am lifting up my voice
With a victory shout.

I refuse to take counsel
From the reasoning of my mind,
But I am commanding everything
That is out of order
To come back into line.

I Will Not

I will not be moved by what I see,
But I am contending for the faith
That was given to me.

I will not be moved by what I feel,
For I know by my spirit
That this is not the real deal.

I will not be moved by what I hear,
And I refuse to live in bondage
To the spirit of fear.

Heavenly Father

Heavenly Father, I cannot add any works
To what You have already done,
For my redemption has been purchased
By the blood of Your dear Son.

Heavenly Father, I cannot add any works
To what You have already done,
So I am thankful for the race
That You daily grace me to run.

Heavenly Father, I cannot add any works
To what You have already done,
So humbly to your throne, I come
To say thank You for the sacrifice
Of your precious Son.

I Am Standing

I am standing in God's righteousness,
And His holy Word I do confess.
I am standing with His belt of truth,
And the Holy Spirit in me is bearing much fruits.

I am standing in His gospel shoes,
And I am confident that I will never lose.
I am lifting up the shield of faith,
And on His promises, I will gladly wait.

I am walking with His helmet on,
And I am tapping into His grace to carry on.
I am fighting daily with the two-edged sword,
And I am declaring that Jesus Christ is *Lord*!

I am praying fervently in the Holy Ghost,
And for more of God's presence,
I will hunger and thirst.

Jesus You Are

Lord Jesus, You are my high tower;
You are my Savior and deliverer.
Lord Jesus, You are my guiding light,
And You are my morning star that shines so bright.

Lord Jesus, You are my prince of peace,
And You are the balm that sets my heart at ease.
Lord Jesus, You are my daily bread,
And You are the Word through which my spirit is fed.

I Declare

I declare that the enemy will not make a mockery
Of the blood that Jesus shed upon Calvary.
The enemy will not make a mockery
Of the stripes that He took when He hung there for me.

I declare that the enemy will not make a mockery
Of the hope and the promises that God has given to me.
The enemy will not make a mockery,
Because the power of Jesus's resurrection
Is working mightily in me.

Your Good Grace

If it had not been for your good grace,
Dear Lord, where would I be?
If it had not been for your good grace,
Life's journey would have been
A very painful race.

Lord, if it had not been for your good grace,
I would have no courage to endure
And keep up with the pace.

Lord, if it had not been for your good grace,
My soul would have been trapped
In a very awful place.

I Am Choosing

I am choosing to walk in the path of love,
And I am seeking for true wisdom
From the Father up above.

I am choosing to walk in the path of peace,
And I am allowing patience to calm me
And keep me at ease.

I am choosing to keep kind words upon my tongue,
And I am praying for God to continually bless me
And keep me strong.

I am choosing to plant seeds of goodness wherever I go,
And God will faithfully supply the water wherever I sow.
I am choosing to offer a soft answer and a gentle touch
In the midst of life's daily hustle and rush.

I am choosing to exercise the power of self-control,
And I refuse to keep digging
Where there is no evidence of gold.

A Steady Stream

Jesus's blood provides a steady stream
That cleanses me and makes me clean.
Jesus's blood provides a steady stream
To the life that He has now redeemed.

Jesus's blood provides a steady stream,
And I am learning daily about the new covenant
And what it means.

Jesus's blood provides a steady stream,
And it makes every mountain much smaller
Than what it seems.
Jesus's blood provides a steady stream,
And His banner of victory is my daily theme.

My Life Is Complete

Through the blood of my Savior,
My life is complete.
And I will never have to stumble
Or experience any defeat.

Through the blood of my Savior,
My life is complete.
For I have found love and forgiveness
At the mercy seat.

Through the blood of my Savior,
My life is complete.
And every need in my life,
He will faithfully meet.

I Discern and See

Lord Jesus, I discern and see
That your sinless body was broken for me.
Lord Jesus, I discern and see
That love is the fulfillment
And faith is the key.

Lord Jesus, I discern and see
That your death bought salvation
And total victory for me.
Lord Jesus, I discern and see
That I am no longer a slave,
But I am totally free.

Your Redemptive Work

Lord, your redemptive work has set me free
From every stronghold of the enemy.
Lord, your redemptive work has set me free,
And sin has no more dominion over me.

Lord, your redemptive work has set me free,
And my spiritual eyes are now open to see.
Lord, your redemptive work has set me free,
And I am walking in your total victory.

My Divine Destiny

I am stepping into my divine destiny,
And I am declaring to the darkness
That I am totally free.

I am stepping into my divine destiny,
And I am walking in the good works
That God has prepared for me.

I am stepping into my divine destiny,
And I am shining like the star
That I was created to be.

A Yielded Vessel

Lord, I am a yielded vessel unto You,
And I am a conduit of your glory
For others to see.

Lord, I am a yielded vessel unto You,
And I am seeking daily for your wisdom
To tell me what to do.

Lord, I am a yielded vessel unto You,
And I am relying upon your grace and mercy
To daily navigate me through.

Lord, I am a yielded vessel unto You,
And I give You all of the glory
And the honor that is due.

I Will Shake Off

I will shake off every attack of the enemy,
And I will successfully fulfill my divine destiny.
I will shake off every attack of the enemy,
And with my mouth,
I will daily confess, declare, and decree.

I will shake off every attack of the enemy,
And I will wage war for the prophecies
That God has been given to me.
I will shake off every attack of the enemy,
And I will walk in the path
That God has chosen for me.

In The Favor

I am walking in the favor
Of my Master and my Savior.
I am walking in His favor,
And my cup is running over.

I am walking in the favor
Of my Master and my Savior.
I am walking in His favor,
And I have grace for every endeavor.

I am walking in the favor
Of my Master and my Savior,
I am walking in His favor,
And this is my greatest harvest ever.

I Break

I break every pattern and cycle of defeat,
And I cast every burden at my Savior's feet.
I break every pattern and cycle of defeat,
And I say yes to my calling,
And I will not retreat.

I break every pattern and cycle of defeat,
And I draw my daily courage and strength
From the mercy seat.

I break every pattern and cycle of defeat,
And I declare that every work of darkness
Is utterly crushed beneath my feet.

I Will Mortify

Every deed of the flesh I will mortify,
And on the strength of my Savior,
I will daily rely.

Every deed of the flesh I will mortify,
And the discipline of God's Word,
I will daily apply.

Every deed of the flesh I will mortify,
And with the life of God's goodness,
I will be satisfied.
Every deed of the flesh I will mortify,
And I will demonstrate a life that is sanctified.

I Am Chasing

I am chasing after my Father's heart,
And in the depth of His wisdom,
I am resting my thoughts.

I am chasing after my Father's heart,
And from the truth of His counsel,
I will never depart.

I am chasing after my Father's heart,
For He has skillfully created
And fashioned every part.

I am chasing after my Father's heart,
For His grace is sufficient
When I am feeling weak
And I have fallen so short.

I Am Resting

Lord, I am resting in the finished work
That You did upon Calvary.
I am resting in your outstretched arms
And your promise to protect me from all harm.

Lord, I am resting in your faithfulness
To deliver my soul from every test.
Lord, I am resting in your perfect peace,
And I pray that in every area of my life,
You will be totally pleased.

I Will Never

I will never conform,
To the ways and patterns of this world,
But on the integrity of God's Word,
I will stand and be bold.

I will never conform
To the ways and patterns of this world,
But I will worship my Savior
From my spirit and my soul.

I will never conform
To the ways and patterns of this world,
But by the renewing of my mind,
I will be daily transformed.

Moving Forward

Lord, I am moving forward by your grace,
And I am drawing strength from the vine
To run and finish my race.

Lord, I am moving forward by your grace,
And I am asking for courage
To deal with every issue that I need to face.

Lord, I am moving forward by your grace,
And I am asking You to help me to steady the pace.
Lord, I am moving forward by your grace,
And I am trusting You
As the Author and Finisher of my faith.

I Am Contending

I am contending for the faith
That was given to me,
And I am looking for all of God's promises
To be daily fulfilled.

I am contending for the faith
That was given to me,
And I am seeking to become all
That God has created me to be.

I am contending for the faith
That was given to me,
And God's power and His glory,
I am determined to see.

I Will Not Be

I will not be a wounded soldier in the fight,
For I am standing in God's strength
And the power of His might.

I will not be a wounded soldier in the fight,
Because I am walking in the Spirit,
And I am guided by His light.

I will not be a wounded soldier in the fight,
Because my heart is to serve God
And do what is right.
I will not be a wounded soldier in the fight,
Because I have found grace and favor in my Father's sight.

The Blood

The blood of Jesus Christ has set me free
From every generational curse and iniquity.
The blood of Jesus Christ has set me free,
And the darkness has no more dominion over me.
The blood of Jesus Christ has set me free,
And I am walking in His joy and victory.

The blood of Jesus Christ has set me free,
And through the eyes of the Spirit,
I am now able to see.
The blood of Jesus Christ has set me free,
And I am walking in the revelation
Of who God has created me to be.

Myself

Lord, I am submitting myself
To your perfect will,
For the true vision for my life,
Only You can fulfill.

Lord, I am submitting myself
To your holy Word
And not to the trivial things
That I have seen and heard.

Lord, I am submitting myself to authority,
But You are the true Master
That is watching over me.

Lord, I am submitting myself
To your heavenly call,
And I am running with endurance
As I give You my all.

Walking and Talking

I am walking and talking with Jesus each day,
And I am asking Him to instruct me
And show me His way.

I am praying and asking for mercy and truth
To build a life that is vibrant
And is bearing much fruits.

I am praying for every hidden darkness
To be swiftly unfold
And that the work of God's kingdom
Will no longer be opposed.

I am praying for the eyes of all nation to see
That there is hope in Christ Jesus,
And there is victory.

I Believe That

I believe that my Savior will see me through,
In spite of the things that I may go through.
I believe that He hears me whenever I plead,
And He will faithfully supply everything that I need.

I believe that He will never leave my side,
For He is the Good Shepherd and my constant guide.
I believe in His power and majesty,
For the witness of His Spirit
Is very strong in me.

I Am Fearless

I am fearless in the face of the enemy's roar,
For his schemes and attacks,
I am not taking anymore.

I am fearless in the face of the enemy's roar,
And I am cancelling his assignments,
And I am shutting every door.

I am fearless in the face of the enemy's roar,
For I am persuaded that through the blood,
My victory is sure.

Stand and Withstand

The enemy will not deceive me
To give up my stand,
For with the blood of Christ Jesus,
I am going to withstand.

The enemy will not deceive me
To give up my stand,
For I am cancelling every evil work
That is coming from his hands.

The enemy will not deceive me
To give up my stand,
For I am walking in Jesus's righteousness,
Knowing that His grace is sufficient
To overcome every test.

The Threefold Blessing

I am walking in the threefold blessing of Abraham,
And I am looking daily to Jehovah
And never unto man.

I am walking in the threefold blessing of Abraham,
And I am refusing to fret over things
That I cannot understand.

I am walking in the threefold blessing of Abraham,
And against the spirit of poverty,
I am taking a righteous stand.

I am walking in the threefold blessing of Abraham,
And I am determine to eat the very best
From the good of the land.

I Am Breaking Through

I am breaking through to recover the spoil,
And I am reaping the harvest
From the years of my toil.

I am breaking through
To the path that is ahead,
And I am speaking new life
To the things that are dead.

I am breaking through
To my divine destiny,
And no weapon that is formed
Will ever stand against me.

You Have Lifted

Lord, You have lifted my soul
From the depth of life's rubble,
And You have been my stronghold
In the days of my struggle.

Lord, You have lifted my soul
From the depth of life's rubble,
And You have totally defeated
Every work of the devil.

Lord, You have lifted my soul
From the depth of life's rubble,
And the blessings in my life,
You have totally doubled.

I Refuse To Compare

I refuse to compare,
And I will not compete,
But I will daily seek a place
At my Savior's feet.

I refuse to compare,
And I will not compete,
For I know that in Christ Jesus,
I have everything that I need.

I refuse to compare,
And I will not compete,
For with Jesus I will never stumble
Or fall from my seat.

I Am Not Playing

I am not playing the role of the victim—
As one without hope—
For I am looking through the lens
Of a much wider scope.

I am not playing the role of the victim—
As one without hope—
But I am drawing strength from my Savior,
And I am learning how to cope.

I am not playing the role of the victim—
As one without hope—
But I am digging both feet in the sand,
And I am holding on to the rope.

I Acknowledge

I acknowledge the Lord
In my going out,
And then in my coming in.

I acknowledge the Lord
On the mountaintop,
And even in the valley of pain.

I acknowledge the Lord
On the stormy sea,
For He was the hand
That was there to deliver me.

I Have Decided

I have decided to rise up
In my level of faith
And honor my Savior
In all of my ways.

I have decided to rise up,
Above the level of complacency,
To walk in the path
That God has set before me.

I have decided to rise up,
Above the moments of fear and doubt,
As I lift up my voice
And give a hallelujah shout.

Faithfully Relying

Lord, I am faithfully relying
Upon your precious blood
And the resurrection power
That has raised You from the dead.

Lord, I am faithfully relying
Upon the integrity of your Word,
And I am tending daily to the soil
Where the good seed has been sown.

Lord, I am faithfully relying
On the soon and coming King
And the mighty cloud of glory
That I know that You will bring.

In This Life

In this life I do not walk alone,
For the Holy Spirit
Will never leave me on my own.

In this life I do not walk alone,
For I have an entrance
That leads up to my Father's throne.

In this life I do not walk alone,
For my heavenly Father is attentive
To my silent groans.

I Believe

I believe in the Creator of the universe,
And what He has ordained,
No man can reverse.

I believe that His Word is infallible,
And nothing with Him is impossible.
I believe that His love is forever strong,
And His blood daily cleanses me of every wrong.

I Am Living

I am living my life
From the inside out,
And I am lifting up a praise
And a victory shout.

I am living my life
From the inside out,
And I am casting down
Every idle thought and doubt.

I am living my life
From the inside out,
And I am making every moment
That I spend with my Savior count.

Overflow

I am living out of the overflow,
And I am finding God's favor
Wherever I may go.

I am living out of the overflow,
And I am planting seeds of goodness
Wherever I may go.

I am living out of the overflow,
For God's unfailing love and faithfulness,
I have truly come to know.

My Hope

My hope lies in Jesus's precious blood,
And not in anything that is man made of.
My hope lies in Jesus, the mediator,
And the one true God who is my Creator.

My hope lies in Jesus's resurrection power
And the grace that He grants me
For every day and every hour.

My hope lies in His infallible Word,
And not in anything that I have seen or heard.
My hope lies in Jesus's soon return
To gather up the saints who are truly His own.

When Fear

When fear comes knocking at my door,
I ask faith to get up and answer it.
When fear comes knocking at my door,
I ask faith to speak God's Word
And settle the score.

When fear comes knocking at my door,
I ask faith to let me to rise up like the eagle
And just begin to soar.

He Is

He is El Elyon, the Most High God;
He is Elohim, the God of power and might.
He is El Shaddai, the mighty God;
He is Adonai, the great Ruler.
And the Holy Spirit is the best tutor.

He is Yahweh, He is Jehovah Lord,
And with Him there is nothing that is too hard.
He is Jehovah Nissi, He is my victory,
And His banner is waving over me.

He is Jehovah Raah, my Good Shepherd,
And He is the greatest guide that I have ever had.
He is Jehovah Rapha, He is my healer,
And the Holy Spirit is the revealer.

He is Jehovah Shammah, He is always there,
And His Holy presence is ever so near.
He is Jehovah Tsikkenu, He is my righteousness.
And my sins, He forgives when I humbly confess.

He is Jehovah Jireh, He provides daily for me,
And all of his blessings, I am able to see.
He is Jehovah Shalom, He is my peace.
And with confidence, I daily rise up
And lie down at ease.

Yes and Amen

When God's Word says yes,
He is not adding any sorrow.
When God's Word says yes,
There is hope for tomorrow.

When God's Word says yes,
He is not adding any stress.
When God's Word says yes,
I can enjoy His sweet rest.

When God's Word says yes,
I can add my Amen
And joyful triumph over every test.

My World

I am framing my world
With the words that I speak,
And with my mouth,
I am daily confessing what I truly believe.

I am framing my world
With the words that I speak,
And I refuse to keep talking
About evil, pain, and defeat.

I am framing my world
With the words that I speak,
And I am listening to the Holy Spirit,
And I am following His lead.

I am framing my world,
With the words that I speak,
And I am expecting a great harvest,
For there is power in the seed.

You have Blessed Me

Lord, You have blessed me in my going out,
And then in my coming in.
You have blessed me in my lying down,
And then in my rising up.

Lord, You have blessed the labor of my hands,
And You have given me the grace
That I daily need to stand.

Lord, You have blessed me far beyond measure,
And your holy Word
Has truly become my greatest treasure.

My Greatest Insurance

Jesus's blood is my greatest insurance policy,
For it will cover me throughout eternity.
Jesus's blood is my greatest insurance policy,
For it protects me from the darkness that I cannot see.

Jesus's blood is my greatest insurance policy,
For when I apply it,
The enemy of my soul will have to flee.
Jesus's blood is my greatest insurance policy,
For it guarantees the fulfillment of my divine destiny.

No More Chains

No more chains are holding me
From becoming all
That my Savior has called me to be.

No more chains are holding me,
Because I am opening my mouth,
And I am making my decree.

No more chains are holding me,
Because the blood of Christ Jesus
Has rendered me totally free.

The Blood of Jesus

The blood of Jesus vindicates me
And gives me boldness to come
And make my decree.

The blood of Jesus vindicates me
From every accusation that the enemy
Will ever bring against me.

The blood of Jesus vindicates me
And protects me from the evil
That I cannot see.

The blood of Jesus vindicates me
And guarantees that my true Advocate
Is always praying for me.

The Enemy

The enemy of my soul
Will not have any hold,
For I refuse to become entangled
With the cares of this world.

The enemy of my soul
Will not have any hold,
For I am a sheep
That is abiding in the Shepherd's fold.

The enemy of my soul
Will not have any hold,
For at the foot of the cross,
I have laid down every load.

Behold the Lamb

I behold the Lamb of God and live,
And all honor and glory,
To my Savior I give.

I behold the Lamb of God and live,
And I am thankful that I am able
To love and forgive.

I behold the Lamb of God and live,
And I am partaking of every blessing
That He so freely gives.

I Am Persuaded

Lord, I am persuaded that for my life,
You have paid the price,
And your blood was the precious sacrifice.

Lord, I am persuaded
That I am born again,
And the Holy Spirit is my special friend.

Lord, I am persuaded that my latter days
Will be more fruitful
In so many ways.

Lord, I am persuaded always
That your light will shine
And the fulfilment of my destiny
Will be right on time.

A Covenant Right

I have a covenant right
To be healed and made whole,
Because Jesus bore the stripes
For my body and soul.

I have a covenant right
To walk in the light,
Because Jesus brought me out of darkness
By the power of His might.

I have a covenant right
To fulfill my divine destiny,
And no work of the enemy
Is going to sabotage me.

You Took

Lord, You took all of the blame,
And You carried my shame
When You died upon Calvary.

Lord, You took all of the blame,
And You carried my shame,
Yet no fault was ever found in You.

Lord, You took all of the blame,
And You carried my shame,
And never once did You attempt
To defend your holy name.

Jesus My Savior

I lift up my hands
And I hold up my head,
Because Jesus, my Savior,
Is alive and not dead.

I lift up my praises
And I give God the glory,
Because Satan is defeated,
And victory is my story.

Only God

Only God can make a way in the wilderness
And forgive our sins
When we humbly confess.

Only God can turn the crooked path to straight
And grant us patience
When we need to wait.

Only God can turn our darkness into light
And deliver us from the terror of the night.
Only God can give us victory in the fight
And deliver us by the power of His might.

I Am Fighting

I am fighting with the blood
And the two-edged sword,
And I am lifting up the name of Jesus,
My redeemer and Lord.

I am fighting with the blood
And the two-edged sword,
And I am keeping my spirit and soul
On the same accord.

I am fighting with the blood
And the two-edged sword,
For a life without productivity,
I can no longer afford.

I Am Lifting Up

Lord, I am lifting up your blood
Against the enemy's attacks,
And I am telling the forces of darkness
That they have to turn back.

Lord, I am lifting up your blood
Against the spirit of fear,
And I am submitting my life
To your total care.

Lord, I am lifting up your blood
Against sickness and disease
Because healing is a benefit of redemption
That I firmly believe and I humbly receive.

Lord You Took

Lord, You took away the pain
And the shame of my youth
When You died upon Calvary.

Lord, You took the rejection
That was meant for my destruction
And You nailed it to the cross.

Lord, You took all of my insecurities,
And You gave me your love and perfect peace.
Lord, You took every drop of tears that I have shed,
And You have given me the fruit of your joy instead.

I Am Never

I am never going back to yesterday
And what my life used to be.
I am never going back to slavery,
Because Jesus Christ has set me free.

I am never going back to the darkness of depression
Or anything that promotes hatred and oppression.
I am never going back to my past history,
For there, I had no real voice or human dignity.

It's King Jesus

It's King Jesus, no matter what or how I feel,
For I know that by His stripes,
That I am totally healed.

It's King Jesus, no matter what I hear or see,
For I know that His blood has totally set me free.
It's King Jesus, in the midst of current affairs,
For I know that my redeemer has a table prepared.

It's King Jesus, regardless of what others may say,
For He is the only one that I daily bow to
In holy reverence and pray.

Poetic Notes from Heaven

My sheep hear My voice, and I know them,
and they follow Me.
—John 10:27

Be Still

Be still and know
That I, your God,
Did sacrifice my Only Son.

Be still and know
That His precious blood
Was the price that He paid for you.

Be still and know
That I have a perfect plan,
And I will give you the grace
That you need to stand.

Not In Vain

Your suffering was not in vain,
For I saw the great glory
That would come from your pain.

Your suffering was not in vain,
For I gave you a Savior,
And I took away your shame.

Your suffering was not in vain,
For to wound and afflict you,
Has never been my aim.

I Am Speaking

I am speaking through the thunder;
I am speaking through the rain.
I am speaking through the thunder,
And even through the pain.

I am speaking through the thunder;
I am speaking through the rain.
I am shaking everything that can be shaken,
And every heart I will awaken.

I am speaking through the thunder;
I am speaking through the rain.
I am speaking loudly through creation,
And my voice will be heard in every nation.

I am speaking through the thunder;
I am speaking through the rain.
I am calling every man to a place of repentance
With a response to their inner conscience.

I am speaking through the thunder;
I am speaking through the rain.
I am fulfilling every Word that I have spoken,
For my greatest desire
Is to heal every heart that is wounded and broken.

Seasons of Distress

There are seasons of distress
That man has not known,
But you must know that I am faithful
To deliver my own.

There are seasons of distress
That man has not known,
But I have given you an entrance
To come up to my heavenly throne.

There are seasons of distress
That man has not known,
But my Spirit is always with you,
And you will never walk alone.

There are seasons of distress
That man has not known,
For my wrath against man's lawlessness
Is really beginning to burn.

The Arm of Flesh

The arm of flesh will fail you,
But in the grip of my grace,
I will hold you.

The arm of flesh will fail you,
But you must walk in the things
That I have shown you.

The arm of flesh will fail you,
But do not let rejection enter your heart,
For it will destroy you.

The arm of flesh will fail you,
But know that my holy presence
Will always be near you.

I Have Raised You

I have raised you up
To be a sheep of my fold,
And I have appointed you to be
An ambassador to the world.

I have raised you up,
And I declare that you are free.
So let your light shine brightly
And bring glory to me.

I have raised you up
To stand firm on my Word,
So lift up your voice loudly,
And let it be heard.

Will You

Will you lay down your life
To follow after Me?
Will you pay the price
To fulfill your divine destiny?

Will you lay down your life
To follow after Me?
Will you still love the ones
Who have wounded and offended you?

Will you pay the price
To die yourself?
Will you live by your faith
And not walk in doubt?

Will you lay down your life
To follow after Me?
Will you walk by my Word
And not what you see?

Will you lay down your life
To follow after Me?
Will you set the wounded ones
And the captives free?

Will you lay down your life
To follow after Me?
Will you cry out for the eyes
Of all nations to see?

Will you lay down your life
To follow after Me?
Will you be the vessel of honor
That I have called you to be?

Stop Fretting

Stop fretting over stuff
That you cannot understand,
And stop bending your ears
To the opinion of man.

Stop fretting over stuff
That you know is not true,
But trust Me to lead you
And show you what to do.

Stop fretting over the state of the economy,
For I have all that you need
For your divine destiny.

Stop fretting over the injustices
That you see in this world,
For I am the Good Shepherd
Who still cares for the sheep of His fold.

The Fallow Ground

I am breaking up the fallow ground,
And I am turning everything in your life around.
I am tearing down the walls
That have you bound,
And soon you will hear a victory sound.

I am breaking up the fallow ground,
And in place of the thorns,
I am giving you a crown.

The Open Door

This is the year of the open door,
For on the wings of the eagle,
I will cause you to soar.

This is the year of abounding grace,
For there is fresh oil for your journey,
And there is inner strength for your race.

This is the year of the open door,
For the cycles of oppression,
You will see them no more.

Remember the Cross

Cast off your cares
And the burden of worry.
And remember the cross
And the pain that I carried.

Cast off your cares
And the burden of worry.
And follow my leading,
And don't be in a hurry.

Cast off your cares
And the burden of worry.
And let Me give you new strength
And a heart that is merry.

Stand

Stand firm upon my written Word,
And cancel every evil report
That you have heard.

Stand strong in the armor
That I have given to you,
And trust the power of my resurrection
To carry you through.

Stand firm when fear comes to assault your mind
And cling to my Word,
For the truth you will find.

Stand strong for the battle is never your own,
But look to the One who still sits on the throne.
Stand firm with the two-edged sword in your mouth,
And trust in Jehovah to work everything out.

Never Be Silent

Never be silent about the promises
That I have given to you.
And never become fearful about what you see,
But bring all of your worries and cares to me.

Never be silent about your blessed hope,
For I have already given you the victory,
And no problem is ever beyond my scope.

Stop

Stop looking at others and comparing yourself,
For you have many gifts and talents
That are just sitting on the shelf.

Stop wearing the dark cloak of pain and regret,
For there is a great land of opportunity
That is waiting for you yet.

Stop trying to be a hero,
And find joy for your sorrow,
For I am your help for today,
And your bright hope for tomorrow.

Open Your Eyes

Open your eyes and you will see
That in prayer, I have made you a VIP.
Open your eyes and you will see
That your victory was won
Upon Calvary's tree.

Open your eyes and you will see
That times of refreshing
Come only from Me.
Open your eyes and you will see
That a child of the King,
I have made you to be.

Each Day

Each day there is grace to start anew,
So forget about the past challenges
That you have been through.

Each day there is grace to start anew.
To accomplish the things
That I have called you to do.

Each day there is grace to start anew,
For the strength of your Savior
Will daily carry you through.

Stay Under

Stay under my blood
In this critical hour.
Stand firm on my Word
And in the strength of my power.

Stay under my blood
In this critical hour,
And look for a sign,
For it is beginning to shower.

Stay under my blood
In this critical hour,
And rely upon my armor,
Like a mighty tower.

The Vision

The vision will surely come to pass,
But you must learn how to trust Me
And do your own part.

The vision will surely come to pass,
And the fruits that you bear,
They will certainly last.

The vision will surely come to pass,
But you must resist every fear and negative thought.
The vision will surely come to pass,
For I am faithful to complete everything that I start.

Never Let

Never let fear and anxiety get you down,
For I have conquered the enemy
And given you a crown.

Never let fear and anxiety get you down,
But always listen for the echo of a victory sound.
Never let fear and anxiety get you down,
For I have sworn by my Word
That I will never let you down!

Go Forth

Go forth and let your light so shine,
And remember that I love you,
And you will always be mine.

Go forth and let my divine wisdom flow,
And trust Me to teach you
What your spirit needs to know.

Go forth and become a true beacon of light,
And let Me strengthen and sustain you
By the power of my might.

Reposition Yourself

Reposition yourself for prosperity,
And tap into the gifts
That I have given to you.

Reposition yourself for prosperity,
And let your life be an example
For others to see.

Reposition yourself for prosperity,
And lay up treasures
That will last for eternity.

Reposition yourself for prosperity,
And place no limits on the person
That I have created you to be.

I Am Calling

I am calling you to come up
To a secret place
Where I can meet with you daily face to face.

I am calling you to come apart
From the cares of this world
And receive a fresh anointing
That is flowing from my throne.

I am calling you to come up
And just rest for a while,
For in my presence, there is a place
Where you are welcome to hide.

The Gatekeeper

I am the gatekeeper of your body and soul,
And there are gifts that I have given you
That you must never withhold.

I am the gatekeeper of your body and soul,
And the fire deep within you,
It must never grow cold.

I am the gatekeeper of your body and soul,
And the anointing that I placed upon you,
It will never get old.

When Life

When life calls you to wrestle,
Do not get caught up in the struggle.
When life looks more like a mountain,
Come and drink from the living fountain.
When prayer feels more like a duty,
Just pause and gaze upon my beauty.

Watch and Pray

This is the hour that I have called you
To watch and pray,
For the Holy Spirit will teach you
And tell you what to say.

This is the hour that I have called you
To watch and pray,
For I am moving in your midst
In a brand new way.

This is the hour that I have called you
To watch and pray,
For you will escape every trap that the enemy lay.

Come Apart

Come apart and relax
In this quiet place,
And let the light of my countenance
Shine brightly on your face.

Come apart and relax
In this quiet place,
And lay down every burden
At the throne of my grace.

Come apart and relax
In this quiet place,
And I will show you how to persevere
And stay strong in your race.

I Am Calling You

I am calling you to walk
In my resurrection power,
For you were created and chosen
For this very hour.

I am calling you to pray
And stand strong in your faith.
I am calling you to come daily
And lay aside every weight.

I am calling you to go forth
And set the captives free;
I am calling you
To bring honor and glory to Me.

I am calling you to serve Me
From the depth of your heart
And trust that I am faithful
To complete what I start.

I Am The

I am the truth,
I am the way.
I have all that you need
For each new day.

I am the life,
I am within.
I have given you everything
That you need to win.

I am the lamp,
I am the light.
I am the One who brings comfort
And make everything right.

I am the joy,
I am the peace.
And my Word has the power
That no enemy can defeat.

Walk in the Light

Step out of the fight,
And walk in the light.
Stand strong in my grace
And the power of my might.

Step out of the fight,
And walk in the light,
And know that the blood of my Son
Has made everything right.

Step out of the fight,
And walk in the light,
And let Me take you from the valley
To a much greater height.

Step out of the fight,
And walk in the light,
For the path of your destiny,
It will surely shine bright.

Do Not Park

Do not park in the valley of Baca,
For there is joy in the Promised Land.
Do not park in the valley of circumstance,
For I am the God of the first
And the second chance.

Do not park in the·valley of self-limitation,
For I am your God
And the Master of all creation.

A True Daughter

You are a true daughter of destiny,
And you are writing a new chapter in history.
You are a true daughter of destiny,
So lift up your voice to declare and decree.

You are a true daughter of destiny,
So walk in your God-given authority,
For I have given you my power and victory.

A Critical Hour

You are living in a critical hour,
But I am Jehovah, your strength
And your mighty tower.

You are living in a critical hour,
So stand firm on my Word,
And don't you ever cower.

You are living in a critical hour,
So keep your lamp trim and ready,
And never unplug from my true source of power.

Arise

Arise from the ashes
And the pain of your past,
And make room to recover
Everything that you have lost.

Arise with the sword of God in your mouth,
And walk in your God-given authority
And start speaking it out.

Arise to your season of Jubilee,
And lift up your eyes
Beyond what you can see.

Arise to your purpose,
You woman of valor,
For I am redeeming the time
In this day and this hour.

I Am Still God

I am still the God of all creation,
And I have a remnant in every nation.
I am still the God of all creation,
And I will extend my mercy
To every tribe and every generation.

I am still the God of all creation,
And I am calling people
To a life of total consecration,
And not a sentence of death and devastation.

Pray

Pray so the enemy will not prey on you.
Pray for my direction,
And I will show you what to do.

Pray for my will to be done in this hour,
For in the prayer of agreement,
There is *dunamis* power.

Pray for the ones
Who are in bondage to sin.
Pray that my desire
Is for all to come in.

Pray for my name
To be exalted on high.
Pray for all of my children
To come and draw nigh.

Behold the Cross

Lift up your eyes
And look to Me,
For my Son, Jesus, paid the price
To set you free.

Lift up your eyes
And behold the cross
Where He carried your sins
And the guilt of your past.

Lift up your eyes
And give glory to Me,
And be the vessel of honor
That I have called you to be.

I Am Releasing

I am releasing a new sound from heaven,
For there will be breakthroughs
That will be greater than seventy times seven.

I am opening new portals of glory,
And I am giving you boldness
To go and declare the gospel story.

I am giving you missiles
That will pierce through the darkness,
For it is time for you to start reaping a bountiful harvest.

It Doesn't Matter

It doesn't matter how you feel,
For in the eyes of your heavenly Father,
You are really a queen.

It doesn't matter what you see,
Just lift up your eyes
And keep looking to me.

It doesn't matter what you have heard,
For you are a child that I love,
And you can always rely upon my Word.

Do Not Focus

Do not focus on your pain
Or your past history,
But just endeavor to fulfill
Your purpose and your divine destiny.

Do not focus on your pain
Or your past history,
But let Me teach you
And unravel the hidden mystery.

Do not focus on your pain
Or your past history,
For my plans for your future
Are total peace and victory.

My Spirit

My Spirit is alive in you
To make you all
That I created you to be.

My righteousness has established you,
In spite of the things
That you have been through.

My glory shall be revealed in you,
And with each step that you take,
I will lead you and show you what to do.

Don't Marvel

Don't marvel at the news of current events,
But walk in my love
And be quick to repent.

Don't marvel at the state of the economy,
For I will supply every need for your family.
Don't marvel at the things that you can see,
For I am your source and your true victory.

Don't marvel at the things that you can hear,
But look to your Savior
And exhibit no fear.

Pray When

Pray when the answer
Seems so far out of sight;
Pray when there are wrongs
That you want Me to make right.

Pray when the darkness
Is all that you can see.
Pray if you are wondering,
Is there victory for me?

Pray when you need wisdom
To know which way to go.
Pray and I will tell you
Everything that you need to know.

Keep Walking

Keep walking on the water,
For you will not sink
Because your faith is so much stronger,
And you are further than you think.

Keep casting your nets,
For I am the keeper of the watch,
And the hand is clearly stating
That you are in for a great catch.

A fishing and a catching
For the souls of men
With my power and anointing
For every wounded soul to mend.

Poems for the Church

And I will give you the keys of the kingdom of heaven, and
whatever you bind on earth will be bound in heaven, and
whatever you loose on earth will be loosed in heaven.
—Matthew 16:19

Lift Up Your Voices

Lift up your voices in one accord,
And saturate the environment
With the praise of the Lord.

Lift up your voices in one accord,
And decree and declare
With the Word of the Lord.

Lift up your voices in one accord,
And tear down every stronghold
That is opposing His will.

Lift up your voices in one accord,
And say yes to Christ Jesus,
Your Savior and Lord.

Let Us Thank God

Let us thank God for kingdom authority,
For favor and divine creativity.
Let us thank Him for overcoming grace
And the wisdom to keep running
In the course of our race.

Let us thank God for the spirit of unity
And a walk that is marked by maturity.
Let us thank Him for a love that is evident to see
And for a church that is known for its productivity.

We Are Blessed

We are blessed to be called children
Of the Most High God.
We are blessed to receive comfort
From His staff and rod.

We are blessed to be called children
Of the Most High God.
We are blessed to live and serve Him
With everything that we have.

Lord Help Us

Lord, help us to be a transformer
And never a conformer.
Lord, help us to be a generation that is resolute,
And help us to stand in your perfect truth.

Lord, help us to be a true representation
Of your family tree,
And help us to walk in your total victory.

Lord, let there be a permanent separation
From the patterns of this world,
And let your resurrection power
Bring a revival to our body and soul.

The Church

The church was created for this very hour
To demonstrate my glory
And the strength of my power.

The church was created for this very hour
To tear down the lies
And the enemy's tower.

The church was created for this very hour,
So lift up your eyes,
For I have delivered you from the enemy's terror.

Lord

Lord, let our hearts and mind be cleaned,
And let us daily walk
As children of the redeemed.
Lord, let our hearts and mind be cleaned,
And let your glory in our lives be visible seen.

Lord, let our hearts and minds be cleaned,
And let your name on this earth
Be always lifted up and highly esteemed.

Step Out

Church, step out of the shadows
And walk in my light.
Walk in my favor
And the power of my might.

Church, step out of the shadows
Into your divine destiny,
For my power and my glory,
I will allow you to see.

Church, step out of the shadows
And take your position,
For this is a time for my people
To make a critical decision.

Your Spiritual Position

Take your spiritual position upon the wall,
And do not be intimidated by the enemy's ploy.
Take your spiritual position upon the wall,
And let your prayers be consistent
As you consecrate your all.

Take your spiritual position upon the wall,
And refuse to come down
Until you have completed your call.

Not the Time

This is not the time for passivity,
But you must use your delegated authority.
This is not the time for passivity,
But you must declare to the darkness
That you are totally free.

This is not the time for passivity,
But you must fight to fulfill your divine destiny.
This is not the time for passivity,
But you must advance in the kingdom
And bring glory to Me.

This Is a Time

This is a time of rest and restoration,
And a life of total consecration.
This is a time of total transformation
For the people of my creation.

This is a time for divine alignment,
And the fulfilment of your heavenly assignment.
This is a time of great prosperity,
And a walk in total victory.

This is a time to lay aside the heavy weights
And make a decision
To walk in the path that is narrow and straight.

Mighty Warriors

Arise you mighty warriors of the King,
And let the heavens thunder
With the worship that you bring.

Arise you mighty warriors of the King,
And honor your Savior
With the praises that you sing.

Arise you mighty warriors of the King,
And give thanks to Jehovah,
For He is getting ready to do a brand new thing.

Help Us to Be

Lord, help us be a light in our community,
And open wide the eyes
That are too blind to see.

Lord, open up the ears
That are too dull to hear,
And call them out of darkness
So they can come and draw near.

Lord, help us to be the salt
That brings seasoning to the lost,
And tell them that their salvation
Was already paid for at the cross.

Your Prodigals

Your prodigals are coming home,
For I have branded them as my very own.
Your prodigals are coming home,
For your cries has come up to the Father's throne.

Your prodigals are coming home,
For I have declared
That your children will no longer roam.

Divine Authority

There is a divine authority
That is given to us in prayer.
And Jesus's blood is the guarantee
That our heavenly Father will always hear.

There is a divine authority
That is given to us in prayer.
And we can come boldly to the Father's throne.
Knowing that He will never deny His own.

There is a divine authority
That is given to us in prayer,
And we will always have an advocate
Who is ready to meet us there.

Father Help Us

Father, help us to finish the race
That You have called us to run.
And let us find strength and courage
Through the blood of Christ, your Son.

Father, help us to finish the race
That You have called us to run.
And let us walk in the victory
That your Son has already won.

Let Your Church

Lord, let your church experience
Your true resurrection power,
And bring down every false and lofty tower.

Lord, let your church experience
Your true resurrection power,
And let there be an outpouring
Of your heavenly shower.

Lord, let your church experience
Your true resurrection power,
And let your Word be our anchor
In this critical hour.

The Hour

This is the hour of declaration
For the people of my creation.
This is the hour of declaration
And a season of preparation.

This is the hour of declaration
And a call for true consecration.
This is the hour of declaration
That I am your true light and your salvation.

You Are

You are God's hands extended
To the lives that are broken.
You are His voice giving hope
Through the gospel that is spoken.

You are God's light on the hill,
And you are in the center of His will.
You are walking in His divine favor,
And your salt will never lose its flavor.

Church Arise

Church, arise and shine,
And let unity be the sign
That you are children of the Most High God.

Church, arise and shine,
And let love be the balm
That brings healing to the body
And keeps the mind calm.

Church, arise and shine,
And walk in your kingdom authority,
For it is a testimony of your faith,
And a mark of your true identity.

Church, arise and shine
To a life of productivity,
For bearing fruits is every believer's responsibility.

Lord Let

Lord, let your church be unified,
And let your name be lifted high.
Lord, let your church be unified
And hearken to our heartfelt cry.

Lord, sanctify us by your truth,
And let godly wisdom be our strong pursuit.
Lord, let Your Word within us take firm root,
And let the Holy Spirit in us bear much fruit.
Lord, hide us from the evil one,
And give us the grace that we need to stand.

There Is

There is a time to pray,
And there is a time to say.
But there is a time
To command things
To get out of the way.

There is a time of peace,
But this is a time of war,
So you better use your spiritual weapons,
Because there is a thief at the door.

Father Ignite Us

Father, ignite us with a holy passion
For the calling to prayer and intercession.
Father, send the former and the latter rain,
And manifest your presence
In the lives of your saints.
Father, let your will on earth be done,
And help us to bring honor and glory to your Son.

Our Hope

Jesus is our hope and our help for tomorrow.
He is the good Shepherd
That we are daily committed to follow.

Jesus is the sunshine
That lights up our world;
He is the true peace and joy
That is deep in our souls.

Jesus is the true anchor
That we steadfastly hold,
For His love and his faithfulness
Will never grow old.

There Is a River

There is a river that is flowing,
From the mercy seat,
And all of God's children
Are invited to meet.

There is a river that is flowing
From the mercy seat,
And we never have to worry
Or experience any defeat.

There is a river that is flowing
From God's mercy seat,
And His power and His glory
Are ever so sweet.

Tear Down

Father, tear down every wall of resistance,
And a fresh flow of your anointing,
Help us now to receive.

Father, tear down every wall of resistance
That opposes your will,
And every cup that is empty,
I ask You now to fill.

Father, tear down every wall of resistance
In the name of your Son,
And give us double grace for the race
That You have called us to run.

It Is Time

It is time for all of God's children
To start seeing eye to eye.
For the gospel of salvation
Is the major reason why.

It is time for all of God's children
To rise up in faith
And possess every one of the enemy's gates.

It is time for all of God's children
To rise up as one
And take the sword of the spirit
And make their command.

God's Watchmen

We are God's watchmen upon the wall,
And His ears are always open
Whenever we call.

We are God's watchmen upon the wall,
And we must never hold our peace
Until we have completed every prayer assignment
And have given it our all.

More Utterances

Lord, I am praying for more utterances
From the Holy Ghost
To be given to your children
As they hunger and thirst.

Lord, I am praying for more utterances
From the Holy Ghost
To teach and supply us
With what we need most.

Lord, I am praying for more utterances
From the Holy Ghost
And for greater visitation
From your angelic host.

We Are Standing

We are standing on God's promises,
And we are daily declaring
That we are His.

We are standing on God's promises,
For Jesus has fatally wounded the enemy's head,
And divine healing is the children's bread.

Sound the Shofar

Lord, sound the shofar in our lives,
And open wide our spiritual eyes.
Lord, sound the shofar
In the year of Jubilee,
And perform your miracle-working power
For all nations to see.

Lord, sound the shofar
In the areas where darkness prevails,
And let the name of the mighty King be hailed.

Lord, sound the shofar
Into every continent,
And call every man and woman
To come quickly now and repent.

Help Us

Lord, help us to walk
As a true soldier of the cross,
And teach us how to rescue
The hurt and the lost.

Lord, help us to run like an athlete
Who will discipline the flesh,
And teach us the true balance
Between meaningful labor and rest.

Lord, help us to be a wise farmer
Who discerns when to plant,
And teach us to gather food in the harvest,
Like the way of the ant.

My Church

I have a need for my church,
In this final hour,
To tear down every false and lofty tower.

I have a need for my church,
In this final hour,
To stand firm on my Word
And cry out for a downpour
Of my heavenly shower.

I have a need for my church,
In this final hour,
To open wide their mouths
To push back the devourer.

Pastor's Prayer

May God strengthen you in the inner man
And multiply the grace
That you need to stand.

May God strengthen you in the inner man
And give you sound wisdom
To perceive and to understand.

May God strengthen you in the inner man
And hold you ever so close
In the grip of His hands.

May God strengthen you in the inner man
And faithfully lead you
In the path of His perfect plan.

Send Your Glory

Lord, send your glory
And fill every room of prayer,
And let your blood cover every saint
That You daily hold so dear.

Lord, send your glory
And fill every room of prayer,
And for every cry of your servants,
Please lend a listening ear.

Lord, send your glory
And fill every room of prayer,
And let every answer from heaven
Be heard in our spirit loud and clear.

We Are Not

We are not living our lives down in Lo Debar,
Because God's work of redemption
Has brought us too far.

We are not living our lives down in Lo Debar,
For Jesus bore our sicknesses,
And He carried every scar.

We are not living our lives down in Lo Debar,
For God's purpose for His church
Is to shine like the star.

We are not living our lives down in Lo Debar,
For we are taking the sword of the spirit
And we are declaring war.

Pastor's Appreciation

Pastor, we are thankful for the Shepherd's heart
That you have shown toward the flock.
We are thankful for the spirit of excellence
That you have set before us as a precedence.
Pastor, we are thankful for your spiritual influence
In shaping lives that will make a difference.

On Behalf Of

Lord, stretch forth your hands
On behalf of your saints,
And lift up the ones
Who are feeling weary and faint.

Lord, stretch forth your hands
To the wounded at heart,
And mend every area
That is broken apart.

Jesus

Jesus is not a babe in a manger
Trying to hide from some danger.
He is no longer on the cross,
Looking down at the lost.

Jesus is not in the tomb,
For there was not enough room
To hold Him in the grave.

Jesus is the man of the hour
Who is still reigning with power.
So look to the horizon,
For it is getting ready to shower.

Printed in the United States
by Baker & Taylor Publisher Services